Arria Sargent Huntington

Under a colonial Roof-Tree

Fireside Chronicles of early New England

Arria Sargent Huntington

Under a colonial Roof-Tree
Fireside Chronicles of early New England

ISBN/EAN: 9783337154172

Printed in Europe, USA, Canada, Australia, Japan

Cover: Foto ©ninafisch / pixelio.de

More available books at **www.hansebooks.com**

UNDER A COLONIAL ROOF-TREE

FIRESIDE CHRONICLES OF EARLY
NEW ENGLAND

BY

ARRIA S. HUNTINGTON

The great eventful Present hides the Past; but through the din
Of its loud life hints and echoes from the life behind steal in;
And the lore of home and fireside, and the legendary rhyme,
Make the task of duty lighter which the true man owes his time
                                                J. G. Whittier

BOSTON AND NEW YORK
HOUGHTON, MIFFLIN AND COMPANY
The Riverside Press, Cambridge
1891

S.G.

CONTENTS AND LIST OF ILLUSTRATIONS.

	PAGE
THE OLD HOUSE . . . . *Frontispiece*	
OUR ANCESTRY OF FREEMEN	1
THE ENTRANCE TO THE WOODS . . .	16
THE SPIRE OF HATFIELD CHURCH	24
A DIARY OF LONG AGO . .	26
THE HOUSE, FROM THE GARDEN	54
THE FAMILY BURIAL-PLACE	80
FIREPLACE IN THE LONG ROOM . . .	102
LATER LIFE IN THE OLD MANSION .	106
APPENDIX	131

UNDER A COLONIAL ROOF-TREE.

OUR ANCESTRY OF FREEMEN.

There has been no nation but, in the beginning of its history, there was the consciousness of a relation to a world which it did not conquer with its swords, and whose fruits it did not gather in its barns nor exchange in its markets. — MULFORD.

IN the spring of 1630, the Winthrop fleet, departing from Plymouth, England, turned its course westward in the direction of the New World. Reaching the coast of the unexplored continent, the first to arrive in Massachusetts Bay was the large ship Mary and John, freighted with one hundred and forty passengers, "godly families and people," under the lead of their two ministers.

These colonists were men and women respectable in condition and lineage, possessed of fortitude, and moved by high moral purpose and strong religious devotion. Of their ten weeks on the ocean one of the number wrote: "So we came by the good hand of the Lord through the deeps comfortably, having Preaching and expounding of the Word of God every day."

At the end of May they found themselves near

the shore; but instead of anchoring in Charles River as was intended, the captain disembarked the whole company in a wild spot at Nantasket, where they were left to shift for themselves. A week later, a day of rest and thanksgiving celebrated their settlement at Dorchester, in which place permanent dwellings were erected during the summer months.

A winter of severe privation followed. Their historian says: "They suffered Hunger and saw no hope in an Eye of Reason to be supplyed, only by Clams and Muscles and Fish. It was not accounted a strange thing in those Days to drink Water and to eat Samp or Hominie without Butter and Milk."

It is related that "a good man, who had asked his neighbor to a dish of clams, after dinner returned thanks to God, who had given them to suck of the abundance of the seas and of treasure hid in the sands."

Even groundnuts and acorns were articles of food, and the Indians who brought their own stores of corn were welcomed as benefactors.

Yet the minds of these high-spirited adventurers were not occupied alone with material necessities or daunted by discomforts. Their deepest concern was for security in political and religious privileges. With their Anglo-Saxon birthright of liberty came a conviction of their right to self-government. The belief of the Puritans in individual responsibility to divine law was intense. To them, the sacredness of personality was embodied in the citizens, or "freemen." Their town and church had been organized on the 20th of March in Plymouth, before the embarkation. Local self-government was thus established and maintained from the first. In defense of it they demanded democratic representation in the Colonial Assembly. A majority under John Cotton favored restricting votes and offices to church members. Three churches, those of Dorchester, Newtown, and Watertown, opposed this "most extraordinary order or law," as it was afterwards characterized by Hutchinson, who adds that "such were the requisites for church membership that the grievances were abundantly greater." Their request was for representation by the towns. When Winthrop maintained "the best part is always the least," Rev. Mr. Hooker argued that "a general council chosen by all is most suitable to transact matters which concern the common good." Mr. Warham and his Dorchester flock held to this principle. Positive in their convictions, resolute in determination, our forefathers were not made of the stuff which yields lightly when liberty is at stake. They looked forth again into the wilderness for an opportunity to found a community under their own charter.

From far away, a hundred miles westward, traders and adventurers brought reports of an open and fertile valley, forests abounding in valuable furs, and a broad and navigable river giving direct communication with the sea. At its mouth Lords Saye and Sele had secured land patents. Above, at Mattaneaug, an outpost was established. Towards this point on Fresh River, now known as the Connecticut, an exploring party proceeded in 1635. It was in the autumn, and a journey through unbroken woodland, over hills and across streams, proved uncommonly arduous. The weather was severe, and the river frozen over in November. The men returned after much suffering. Nevertheless their report was so far satisfactory that in the following year the whole of Rev. Mr. Warham's church removed thither with their pastor. Under his lead they made a settlement at what is now known as Windsor, Connecticut. Already Pynchon, with a colony from Roxbury, had become established higher up the river, at Agawam. A large company came from Cambridge, then called Newtown, with their minister, Mr. Hooker. Hartford and Wethersfield formed part of this active and hopeful community, and in 1636 a General Court was instituted. At that gathering Mr. Hooker maintained that " the foundation of authority is laid in the free consent of the people."

The Constitution then adopted by the freemen of the three towns was the " first known to history that created a government, and it marked the beginnings of American democracy." Its federation of independent towns, its extended suffrage, the different form of representation in the Assembly and the upper House, all formed a republican government similar to that adopted later by the United States.

To such brave men as those who embarked in the Mary and John, who founded the Dorchester township and established the State of Connecticut, we owe the grand ideas of the nation as the realization of freedom, the sovereignty of the people, and the sacredness of their rights. Self-taxation, trial by jury, and the office of justice of the peace represented to them the institution and preservation of personal liberty.

A quarter of a century passed away, and great events had taken place across the sea. The King of England had ruled without a Parliament, and Parliament had ruled without a king. The reign of Charles I. and the Protectorate of Cromwell were alike over. Both men were in their graves and another Stuart was restored to the throne.

The young and vigorous life of the new country felt but lightly the strain of changes which had so profound an effect in the Old World. The tide of colonization had been checked with the ascendency of the Puritans during the Commonwealth. The settlers occupied themselves in strengthening their local government, forming a federated league, uniting in defense against the Indians, clearing and improving their lands.

Religious affairs were a matter of deep concern. At a council in Boston in 1660, dissension arose on the subject of baptism, and other questions involved in what was known as "The Half-way Covenant." The majority advocated admitting the children of professing Christians not in full communion with any one particular church. In the Hartford colony serious division occurred. Rev. John Russell and many of his flock believed that the Congregational policy was seriously threatened. The result was, that again a pastor and people sought a new home, and in that same year laid out the town of Hadley, across the Massachusetts line. About twenty miles above Pynchon's settlement they found a wide valley of unusual loveliness, with great advantages of soil and surroundings.

A mountain chain rises here abruptly from the meadow-land, closing in the rich intervale. The Connecticut, in its southward course, before entering the narrow opening between opposite peaks, takes a sweep through a broad basin, which, long before the memory of man, was washed by alluvial deposits. Natural terraces rise from the banks to wooded highlands east and west. Even when encircled by primeval forest, this open valley must have had its own charm for those who recalled the peaceful scenery of Old England. Native elms stood here and there in the green meadows, groups of walnut trees followed the brooks. The silver stream, its gentle current unbroken by rocks or rapids, was bordered by sparkling sands and rich verdure.

In such surroundings the new town was begun. Its generous plan may have been in remembrance of the good old times when every English village had its common, before the inclosures of later years had robbed the poor man of his birthright. The founders of Old Hadley laid out its broad street sixteen rods wide, leaving in the centre a strip of grass where village cows and geese could roam. It stretched from bank to bank of the great river curve, five miles in length, which incloses the meadow-land. English elms, patriarchs to-day, were planted in a double row along the highways bordering the green, and bestowed upon the village a wealth of shade which has made it the pride of the country-side. Spacious houses were erected on the street; pasture land for common use inclosed on the edge of the wilderness; a meeting-house was erected, and the government of the town established, in the free and independent form already dear to the colonist.

The river, navigable at the time for good-sized boats, formed a means of communication with the towns below.

Fertile fields, abundant forests and streams, furnished support to a hard-working and frugal population. Openings for trade were developed.

Had it not been for the Indian atrocities which struck terror to all unprotected villages, peace and prosperity would have prevailed.

King Philip's War burst upon New England with fire and sword. The towns planted along the Connecticut suffered most.

In connection with one of these attacks, that picturesque event occurred which has made Hadley memorable. Tradition tells that one of those fasts, common at that period in any time of public peril, had called together all the inhabitants in the meeting-house. This building stood in the middle of the green. While all were engaged in prayer, a band of Indians stealthily approached the place, and discovered how favorable was the opportunity for an attack. Not a breath of suspicion disturbed the devout congregation within. But one eye, alert and trained in military service, detected the advance of the savages. An alarm was sounded, and as the men rushed in confusion from the church they found at their head, in command, a stranger, "a grave, elderly person, in his mien and dress different from the rest of the people. He not only encouraged them to defend themselves, but put himself at their head, rallied, instructed, and led them to encounter the enemy, who by this means were repulsed." Suddenly as he had appeared the stranger vanished. In the hurry and confusion, the brief alarm and sudden relief, only one explanation could be found for the apparition. As "the Angel of Hadley" he was long referred to. It was many years later that the fact for the first time became known that, in the house of old Parson Russell, two of the judges of Charles I. had been concealed. There seems little doubt that it was Goffe, the younger of the two, who saved the village on this occasion. To the brave old minister who risked so much to afford them shelter, there must have seemed after this event a special significance in the admonition, "Be not forgetful to entertain strangers, for thereby some have entertained angels unawares." Goffe and Whalley left England before Charles II. was proclaimed king, but heard of his restoration when they arrived at Boston. A pardon was at first expected, and they were honorably received by Governor Endicott. Whalley was a cousin of Cromwell, and one of his lieutenant-generals. Goffe, who married his daughter, was a major-general. Both men were distinguished for firmness, courage, and religious devotion.

When it appeared that their names were not included in the act of indemnity it was no longer safe for them to remain at large in the colonies. Warrants were issued, and two young and zealous royalists undertook to apprehend them. A thorough search was made along the western frontier, and while they were under Parson Russell's roof inquiry was made there for them. There is some suspicion that in this case their pursuers were not eager to find them, for tradition has it " that they sought as those who sought not."

Their first refuge with Parson Davenport, of New Haven, soon became known, and threatened danger to him. To clear him of further question the regicides showed themselves publicly, and then found concealment in a cave in the neighborhood. Here some Indians came upon their traces and they were again in peril. Rev. John Russell, probably through his friend Mr. Davenport, had already offered them a hiding-place, and his home, at a hundred miles' distance, was comparatively remote. Thither they made their way, traveling by night, and arriving October 13, 1664. This was only two years after the town was settled, and they remained there certainly till 1679. The last record of Goffe is a letter written on April 2d, and dated " Ebenezer," the name which he always gave to his place of refuge. Governor Hutchinson, in his " History of Massachusetts Bay," mentions that Dixwell also, another of the judges who took refuge in the colonies, was for a short time concealed at the parsonage.

Hutchinson had in his possession Goffe's diary, kept while at Hadley, which recorded every little event which occurred in the church and among the village families. This document would be now of great value, but it was burned at the time the governor's library was destroyed by a mob. A letter written to Goffe from England, by his wife, is described by Palfrey as "tender, magnanimous, and devout, scarce to be read without tears."

It is supposed that Whalley died while at the parsonage, and was interred in the cellar. As late as the end of the next century, Dr. Dwight mentions that he had talked with a man who discovered there human remains while removing a wall. The chamber in which the refugees lived so long had secret access above and below, so that escape might be made either way. The frame of the building, now converted into a tavern, is still pointed out on the broad village street.

It was in September, 1679, that the rescue at Hadley took place. The first written account of it is found in a foot-note to Hutchinson's History. He there says: "I am loath to omit an anecdote handed down through Governor Leverett's family. I find Goffe takes notice in his journal of Leverett's being in Hadley."

The romance of the event attracted the fancy of Sir Walter Scott, and he describes it at length, with many details manifestly incorrect, through the mouth of Major Bridgenorth, in "Peveril of the Peak." The most serious mistake is that in which he makes Whalley and not Goffe the hero of the adventure. As relatives and companions, the confusion might easily occur; but the date settles the matter, as, according to Stiles's "History of the Three Judges," Whalley was superannuated in 1675. Scott in a note refers to Cooper's use of the incident in "The Wept of Wish-ton-Wish." It was probably many years after Parson Russell's death that his share in the concealment of the regicides became known. The stanch old Puritan was buried in the graveyard (then new, now covered with moss-grown slabs) of the town which he had assisted to lay out. Over his resting place is a large tablet, formed of the soft red sandstone of the district, and inscribed in the rude style of those times.

Whether the secret he carried so long was ever committed to paper by him is not known, as the village records were afterwards destroyed in the burning of the parsonage. The story of Goffe's apparition, however, remains as an unquestioned tradition in the community. A descendant, born in the house with which these chronicles are associated, remembers hearing it in his youth from an old man who had held the legend since his own boyhood, and whose grandfather must have been living when the mystery was first revealed.

In this same homestead the story was in all probability directly transmitted from an authentic source, inasmuch as its first occupant was a granddaughter of Parson Russell's third wife, Phœbe

Gregson. She was the daughter of a citizen of New Haven, active in the planting of the colony, and interested in promoting its prosperity through trade with England. For that object he took passage with others appointed to secure royal patents. The vessel was never again heard from, but tradition runs that it was seen as a spectre ship in New Haven harbor, after a prayer-meeting held in behalf of the crew.

Phœbe became the wife of Rev. John Whiting, who graduated from Harvard College in 1668. His father, William Whiting, had been treasurer of the Hartford colony, and there his son's pastorate was spent. Phœbe was his second wife, and after his death became the third wife of Parson Russell, whom she survived for many years. She removed to her early home, New Haven, to the house of her son Joseph. It is probable, however, that associations with Hadley were always kept up, as her step-daughter married a son of Parson Russell, and in the next century her grand-daughter came there as a bride. This Elizabeth was the daughter of Elizabeth Whiting, whose parents were Phœbe and the Reverend John. She married Nathaniel Pitkin, the son of William Pitkin, a leading man in the Hartford colony and the founder of the family in this country. In the genealogical history of his descendants, a copy is given of a letter, still preserved, which was written to him from England in 1667. It is addressed as follows: —

ffor
William Pitkin at
Hartford Town neare
neare Conēticut river
Leave this with Mr. Thomas
Smyth neare the Spring
in Boston
in New England

This spring, the same which was flowing at the time the new post-office was built, was in Spring Lane, near Governor Winthrop's house. It is thus pleasantly described by Duke. He speaks of "the ancient Spring-gate, the natural fountain at which no doubt Madam Winthrop and Anne Hutchinson filled their flagons for domestic use. The gentlemen may have paused here for friendly chat, if the rigor of the governor's opposition to the schismatic Anne did not forbid. The hand-maid of Elder Thomas Oliver, Winthrop's next neighbor on the opposite corner of the Spring-gate, fetched her pitcher, like another Rebecca, from this well. Grim Richard Brackett, the jailer, may have laid down his halberd for a morning draught."

In the will of Nathaniel Pitkin this quaint provision is made: "And whereas there is in my possession one great brass kettle, one two-eared silver cup, and divers other things, all of which may be found entered in a small paper book, folio 2, which said goods were never my estate, but were given by my honored mother-in-law Mrs. Russell, deceased, to my daughter Elizabeth Pitkin, which said goods I desire my wife to take into her care in trust for my said daughter," etc.

This brass kettle must have gone with his daughter to her new home, for it may be seen to this day under the eaves of the house which was built for her, carefully preserved among many other relics.

Of her arrival at Hadley as a bride, a story is told which illustrates customs of that time. Coming from Hartford, the young couple were met at Mountain-gate, the entrance into the valley, by a party of welcome from the village. One of the youths by some artifice persuaded her to mount the pillion of his horse, and then leaping on before, he rode off with his prize, accomplishing the trick of "stealing the bride," much to the confusion of the lady who was thus introduced to her new home.

Her husband, who is described as of a "mirthful but devout disposition," probably entered into the spirit of this rude pleasantry. He was the great-grandson of one of the founders of the town, which had now nearly reached its first century of existence. John Porter was a Windsor colonist, and served as grand juror and recorder. His son Samuel, in the settlement of Hadley, was assigned a valuable lot in the centre of the village. He is mentioned in the record of the General Court as "having been assiduous in caring for wounded persons during the Indian wars, giving much himself for the purpose."

He was a Justice of the Peace, the first of a long line in the town of the same family who held that office for two hundred years. This is an honorable distinction for any lineage to possess, as it implies faithfulness to the interests of the community and the confidence of the public. Humble as the service may seem, it has been said of it that "it embodies perhaps the highest conception in the Anglican civil system. It represents the peace of society as conditioned in justice, and there was a deep significance in the formula in which the old writs ran, 'in the peace of God and the Commonwealth.'"

The second Samuel grew up to be an extensive trader, leaving behind him "the immense estate of £10,000." The wedding of his son Aaron, a minister, is described by Chief Justice Sewall in his diary.

The early Porter residences were all in the broad village street. But when young Moses looked about for a place to establish himself, he selected a spot two miles northward. Up to this date, fear of the Indians had prevented the inhabitants of the valley towns from building outside the settlements. Stockades for defense had been abandoned, but fields could not be cleared or labor done with safety. Attacks of the Cana-

THE ENTRANCE TO THE WOODS

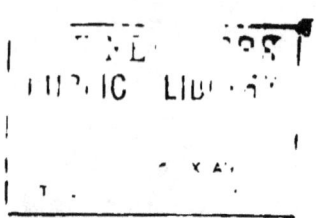

dians and savages were made when least expected. Between the Connecticut and Lake George were as yet no habitations.

By the year 1752, security seemed to be assured. Two miles above Hadley meeting-house lay a common pasturage, fenced across at the north and south, with gates at the highway. The river formed one boundary, and on the east a deep ditch was dug at the edge of the clearing, to prevent the cattle from straying into the wilderness. Traces of this trench are still plainly to be seen back of "Pleasant Hill."

The meadow known as "Forty Acres," but in fact considerably larger in extent, became open to purchase, with the rest of the inclosure. Such a sheltered intervale offered many charms for a permanent dwelling-place.

Through chestnut slopes descending from Mt. Warner, clear streams found their way to the broad river, navigable for various kinds of craft and abounding in fish. Arable land, enriched each year by the spring freshets, rolled in smooth undulations back to the woodland. Lofty trees stood here and there among the verdure, and waving willow and maple fringed the sloping shore. In the distance could be seen the bold outlines of successive ranges of hills towards the setting sun, and the misty peaks of the Green Mountains.

In such surroundings one is reminded of the lines : —

> "Peace trills in the songs of the valleys,
> And freedom blows from the hills."

From her Hartford home to so secluded a spot must have been a change to Elizabeth Pitkin. There were no dwellings between there and the village. The nearest houses were across the river at Hatfield. There, in the century before, one of the most unexpected attacks of the Indians had been made. On a lovely September day, while the men were harvesting corn in the meadows, a band of savages attacked the houses outside the stockade, and carried away to Canada twenty-one people, mostly women and children. Their long and painful march through the chill autumn weather, the vicissitudes of the brave scouts who followed them through bitter frost and peril of starvation, form a thrilling tale of adventure. They were brought back the following spring with rejoicing through all the country, a party going towards Albany to meet them.

Two children, born in exile, and named Captivity and Canada, grew up to womanhood, and their descendants and those of other captives are still living in the village.

Although, by the year 1765, direct depredations from the north had ceased in this neighborhood, uneasiness was felt along the frontier at the disposition of the French to encroach on the territory of the British Colonies. To defend its possessions, the mother-country sent over General Braddock.

In the campaign that he inaugurated, an attack on Crown Point was one of the four lines of military strategy contemplated. For this enterprise Massachusetts was ready with her volunteers, and 4,500 men enlisted.

Among other troops sent from New England, Israel Putnam was private in a Connecticut regiment, and John Stark, afterwards the hero of Bennington, accompanied the Green Mountain recruits.

Parkman thus describes the men who went forth to encounter the disciplined ranks of the French regulars, and the fierce and treacherous warfare of their savage allies: —

"These soldiers were no soldiers, but farmers and farmers' sons, who had volunteered for the summer campaign. One of the corps had a blue uniform faced with red. The rest wore their daily clothing. They had no bayonets, but carried hatchets in their belts as a sort of substitute. At their sides were slung powder-horns, on which, in the leisure of the camp, they carved quaint devices with the points of their jack-knives. They came chiefly from plain New England homesteads, — rustic abodes, unpainted and dingy, with long well-sweeps, capacious barns, rough fields of pumpkin and corn, and vast kitchen chimneys, above which, in winter, hung squashes to keep them from frost, and guns to keep them from rust."

Moses Porter received a commission as captain of a Hadley company. One of the village boys, who saw him in his officer's uniform, was so impressed with his appearance that he told the tale in after years of how Captain Porter marched away to the wars. But it was a lonely and sorrowful home which was left behind. In letters written to him in camp, his wife speaks of the dark face of some wandering Indian seen occasionally at night pressed against the window pane. Remembering that it was against these wily foes that her husband was fighting, it must have given her a thrill of apprehension.

It was only three years after the building of their house that Captain Porter was called away. In September, 1755, occurred the battle at Crown Point.

The British troops were under the command of General Johnson; their adversaries were led by Dieskau. About eight o'clock on the morning of the 6th, the encounter took place. Parkman gives a vivid description of the fatal scene. Speaking of the troops under Dieskau he says:—

"They moved rapidly on through the waste of pines, and soon entered the rugged valley that led to Johnson's camp. At their right was a gorge, where, shadowed by bushes, gurgled a gloomy brook; and beyond were the cliffs that buttressed the rocky heights, seen by glimpses between their boughs.

On the left rose gradually the lower slopes of West Mountain. All was rock, thicket, and forest. There was no open space but the road along which the Regulars marched, while the Canadians and Indians pushed their way through the woods in such order as the broken ground would permit.

They were three miles from the lake when their scouts brought in a prisoner, who told them that a column of English troops was approaching. Dieskau's preparations were quickly made. While the Regulars halted on the road, the Canadians and Indians moved to the front, where most of them hid in the forest among the slopes of West Mountain, and the rest lay close among the thickets on the other side.

Thus, when the English advanced to attack the Regulars in front, they would find themselves caught in a double ambush. No sight or sound betrayed the snare; but behind every bush crouched a Canadian or a savage, with gun cocked and ears intent, listening for the tramp of the approaching column.

In the British van were their allies, the Mohawks. It is said that Dieskau's Iroquois, seeing their relations, wished to warn them of their danger. If so, the warning came too late. The muskets on the left blazed out a deadly fire and the men fell by scores. In the words of Dieskau, the head of the column 'was doubled up like a pack of cards.',

The men in the rear pressed forward to support their comrades, when a hot fire was suddenly opened on them from the forest along their right flank. Then there was a panic; some fled outright, and the whole column recoiled. The van now became the rear, and all the force of the enemy rushed upon it, shouting and screeching.

There was a moment of total confusion, but a part rallied, fighting behind trees like Indians, and firing and falling back by turns, bravely aided by some of the Mohawks and by a detachment which Johnson sent to their aid. 'And a very handsome retreat they made,' writes Seth Pomeroy, of Northampton, 'and so continued till they came within about three quarters of a mile of the camp.'

So ended the fray long known in New England fireside story as 'The Bloody Morning Scout.'"

Among those who fell, tradition says by the hand of an Indian, was Moses Porter.

Six days later the news reached Hadley. No relic of the officer but his sword was ever returned. His body was left among the slain; a gravestone in the village burying-ground bears the date of his death. When the mortal remains of Elizabeth Porter were taken from the home where she had lived a widow for forty-three years, they were placed in a boat, rowed down the silent river, and laid beside that stone. The shadow of her early grief never left her. She bore always a saddened aspect and a sorrowing heart. We find her mother's grave between the family lot and the tombstone of Parson Russell, her stepfather. By the date it appears that she, also, was taken soon after the homestead was built. Orphaned and alone, the widow was left with the care of her young daughter and the management of a large estate.

We can easily form a picture of their home. The house, although enlarged and improved at various times in later years, was originally of ample size. Its main structure bore the same features as at the present day, excepting that the gambrel roof was added in the next century. The style was similar to that of the old family mansions in Hadley Street. A broad hall, with an open stairway leading to the floor above, divided good-sized rooms on either hand, a " parlor bedroom," and the " Long Room," only used for state occasions. Another hall at a right angle led to the little door-yard filled with lilacs and syringas.

This south entrance had its flagged walk, and small gate opening into a large space where carriages drove up. The front door, with its big brass knocker, was seldom used; the grass grew close up to the steps of the white porch. In a wing at the rear stood a huge chimney, occupying space enough for a small room, with great fireplace and ovens. Another large chimney was erected when the present kitchen, cheese-room, etc., were added.

An inclosed piazza, with seats along the sides, known as the "stoop," extended along the whole western length of the house. In harvest time a long table was set there for the reapers. All through the summer the churning, washing, and other household work were there carried on. At nightfall it afforded a grateful retreat after the labors of the day.

To those of later generations it has been a favorite social gathering-place at that hour. Then the mist deepens in the quiet meadows as the crimson glow fades in the west. In the village across the river, the slender spire stands out distinct against the sky. Through the stillness we may hear the tread of horses' hoofs crossing the bridge by the mill a mile away. The clear notes of the thrush sound from the trees along the shore. The Whately hills grow dark in the twilight, the first star appears above the elm-trees. On a Sunday evening, or a prayer-meeting night, come across the water the harmonious accents of a church bell.

"When the old bell spoke to us, it was mostly on grave themes. Its voice was always the same, solemn, tender, peaceful, and to me inexpressibly sweet. It was a perpetual monitor speaking to our higher nature. How many times I have sat

THE SPIRE OF HATFIELD CHURCH

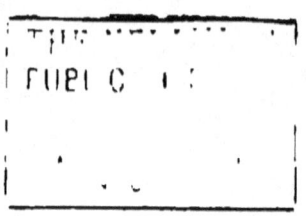

in the old stoop, spell-bound after the tolling began, until its last note had ceased. I used often to get my sermon before others had begun to listen. I had a fancy that the water lent a liquid softness to the tones which they would not otherwise have had. If I was harassed and vexed with cares, it bade me be calm and patient; to passion it said peace. When in melancholy moods its song was one of hope. If I were becoming absorbed in a mere worldly life, a single note, lightly heeded, would be enough to prove its emptiness and vanity."

The house was placed some rods back from the highway on a little knoll. An orchard and garden were laid out on the north, and shade-trees planted in front. Between the great barn, with its various outbuildings, and the dwelling, was left a wide grassy space which has been for generations shaded by magnificent elms. Between that and the street a large sheep-yard was inclosed. Green meadows stretched to the river, and pasture and woodland abounded in the opposite direction.

It was such an estate, sufficient for a comfortable support, yet requiring care and superintendence, which was left to the widow and her young daughter.

A DIARY OF LONG AGO.

Old events have modern meanings ; only that survives
Of past history which finds kindred in all hearts and lives.
JAMES RUSSELL LOWELL.

NOTHING appeals more quickly to sentiment, or awakens a deeper spirit of reflection, than to peruse the actual record of past life written in the faded ink of bygone years, phrased in the quaint langage of an earlier time, and registered with the unconsciousness of a private journal. Such a manuscript, written in a close, stiff hand, on pages yellow with age and stitched together in home-made brown-paper covers, was found stored away under the garret eaves of the old roof-tree. Five volumes cover the record of forty-nine years, from girlhood to old age. Beginning at sixteen, Elizabeth Porter kept for nearly half a century a weekly chronicle, written on Sunday and giving a sketch of the events of the preceding week. She invariably set down the text of the sermon she had heard, sometimes by chapter and verse, in later years copied in full with some short account of the discourse.

The first date is October 16, 1763, the last April 5, 1812. Brief as are the weekly entries, they convey very perfectly an impression of life in the colonial times, during the Revolution, and in the period following.

The opening pages, penned by a young girl just developing into womanhood, give a pleasant picture of neighborly life. Although the home was in a solitary situation, and the mother a saddened widow, the days were not lacking in variety. Kinsfolk in the village seem to have been full of kindly interest in the fatherless child. There were cousins at three houses,—the squire's, the lawyer's, and the parson's. These households are constantly mentioned. The wife of lawyer Porter was a daughter of Jonathan Edwards. This and other connections gave the advantage of the best society of those days.

The mode of intercourse seems far simpler and more unconstrained than at the present time. Acquaintances rode from town to town and stayed for a whole day, entering into the homely occupations of the family.

April 22, 1767. "Came here Miss Pen and Miss Polly to help me quilt a dark brown quilt."

May 26. "We received a visit from Mr. Jewet and his son, with divers others that waited on them."

June 16. "For the afternoon, Polly and Sally Williams came here, and we all went strawberrying."

Wednesday she again went for strawberries.

Thursday she watched with a sick man in the village.

Wednesday, July 26, was a quilting. Thursday a huckleberrying. The next week another quilting. Visitors come and go, among them "Miss Biah Chapin, a pretty young woman from Springfield." Friends from a distance come and "tarry" for a while. Miss Polly is often mentioned. Other names are characteristic of a period long passed, — Experience, Dorcas, Abigail, Salome, Tabitha, Submit, Jerusha, Electy, Thankful. On one occasion we find the suggestive record, "Silence went home and Patience came."

In November begin the singing meetings, at that time the favorite recreation of the young people during the winter. In a community where neither cards or dancing were ever heard of, this diversion was very popular.

February 14, 1768, comes a "singing lecture. A great many strangers attended it and very much applauded it. After meeting, drank tea at Esquire Porter's with a large number of ladies."

Social occasions at home and abroad occur with frequency through the cold weather. Companies from the neighboring towns are hospitably received.

Of one of the formal tea-drinkings a grandson has written out his recollections: —

"One might infer that at this period, when the Puritan element still prevailed with considerable rigor, Thanksgiving being over, there would not be much to break in upon the monotony of the long winter months. This, however, was not the case. Winter was the time for making tea parties on a large and generous scale. They were not like our modern receptions, where seats are supposed to be a superfluity; or like our sociables, when people are invited to meet together and pay for the entertainment. The old-fashioned tea party, in order to go off well, must not number less than ten or fifteen couples. We were living two miles out, so some one must be sent the day before to give the invitations. Many were the discussions and consultations in respect to the weather, for if a storm should intervene there would be great danger of failure. What a relief it would have been if in those days we could have had the advantages of the weather bureau! Many a tempest in a teapot, as well as on the sea, might have been avoided if our grandmothers had only enjoyed the benefits of this achievement of modern science. They had Thomas's Almanac, to be sure, but what could Thomas do as a weather prophet in the face of the weather bureau? His genius would certainly have paled before the stern deductions of facts and figures. But the men were close observers of the weather, and when they reported the heavens favorable it generally proved so. Many a time have we stood in the old 'space' fronting the road and listened for the bells, and strained our eyes, in the duskiness of coming evening, to catch sight of the first gay 'cutter' with its complement of rosy faces, buffalo robes, hoods, caps, etc. And how our pride was touched if the guests came slowly, and there was fear lest all the hitching-posts would not be occupied! But they continued to come until the large parlor, which was called the 'Long Room,' was completely filled with as good-looking and contented a company as often get together in a country village. Of course there were no centre-table or gaslights, but there were candles on the mantels and on the two small tables, one at each end of the room. And besides there was the old fireplace with its big andirons, its two backlogs and forestick, filled between with smaller wood, glowing like a furnace, crackling and roaring as if in very mirth in anticipation of the festive hours that were to follow.

The fashion was to send tea round. This was a most orderly proceeding, and was a good test of the executive ability of the hostess. It took a strong and trusty hand to carry the large waiter with its precious burden of old-time chinaware filled to the brim with the beverage that 'cheers but not inebriates.' As it is ushered in, there is a pause in the hum of voices. The salver is rested for a moment on a small table while the minister or some other saintly person asks a blessing on the food. Then the hum goes on with renewed vigor. The tea is passed; buttered biscuit and cakes, with the etceteras of the tea-table, follow, occupying about an hour or so, after which the company change their seats, assorting themselves sometimes into groups, as inclination suits, so preparing themselves for the evening's gossip (I use this in a good sense, of course), or to discuss more profitable themes, as it suits them. A shorter interval of apples and nuts later in the evening, but before nine o'clock, finishes the entertainment. The horses are at length brought out, impatient with their long waiting in the cold. We can hardly hold them until the sleigh receives its load, and at the given signal they dash off to the music of merry bells and creaking snow; the weird light of the moon, as they ride homeward, throwing snowdrifts, the gaunt trees and their shadows, and straggling fences, into a thousand shapes. Soon they are all gone, the last notes of the bells are lost in the distance, and we hurry into the old parlor to enjoy its unwonted light. We pull away the fender, and for a little while bathe ourselves in the warmth and comfort of the great fire, which is slowly spending itself, but whose embers still glow and gleam as if theirs had been the scene of some grand holocaust. To the younger part of the family at least, and quite likely to the older ones also, this is the most enjoyable part of the evening. We gather into a closer circle, and discuss again the news of the neighborhood and other small-talk of the departed guests. But the evening wanes, the frosty winds are pushing at the windows, the flickering shadows on the walls remind us that bedtime is at hand. Reverently the prayer is offered; we scatter for the night, leaving the old room to its accustomed silence and darkness.

The old-time life, looking at it from my standpoint and in its better aspects, — how simple and yet how grand it was!"

The frequent social occasions did not interfere with the household work, in all of which the heads of the family bore an active part. The substantial material for clothing was manufactured in the house, and all the garments were cut and made under the supervision of the itinerant workwomen who were such a feature in the life of those days.

"Rene Parsons came here to make the girls' surtouts."

"Mrs. Rebekah D. came here to talor; tarried till Friday."

"Lodemy came to weave."

"Mrs. H. here to weave our camblet."

A wedding outfit included the making of a "copperplate bed-quilt."

On a visit to Boston a dressmaker is called in "to make my dress plumb."

Two or three times a week she "rides into town of arrands." There she also lends a hand at quiltings. At the parsonage she helps quilt "a black cassimere coat for the minister's wife."

The first break in this homely, quiet life occurs in 1768, when Elizabeth was twenty-one. In the month of May her cousin, Squire Porter, took a party of four to Boston, including his wife, his sister Miss Polly, and herself.

Although the first of many visits, it must at this time have seemed a great event to one brought up in the seclusion of an isolated farm.

The diary runs: "Got boarding at one Mrs. Baxter's. Saw the great carryings-on at election. Went to Trinity Church. Heard one Mr. Kneeland. Monday, Nehemiah W., who belongs to Cambridge College, came over to Boston, got a chaise, and waited on us to Roxberry."

This ride in a chaise was quite a circumstance to those who had hitherto made all expeditions in the saddle or on a pillion. The journey of a hundred miles from Hadley could at that time be taken in no other way.

Tuesday they went to Cambridge in company with their cousin, Lawyer Porter, who had joined the party.

"Dined at Bradliffe's and drank tea in one Jonathan Smith's chamber, who belongs to this town. Mr. Phillips, of Boston, with his wife and two sisters, Miss Polly and Miss Nabby, they met us at Cambridge by tea-time; all drank tea together."

This Mr. Phillips is worthy of notice. President Dwight says of him: "At the age of twenty-one he persuaded his father and uncle to make the extensive benefactions which founded both the academies at Andover and Exeter. Of this property he was the natural and presumptive heir. He was an only son, and his uncle, who had no child, regarded him with parental affection. In an important sense, therefore, the property thus given was all his own."

The party returned home after a week's sight-seeing and visiting.

The next month, June 26th, Elizabeth went to a quilting in the village, followed by a strawberrying. Among the company the name of her future husband is mentioned for the first time: "Charles Phelps took Lawyer Porter's wife in a chair." A riding-chair was a chaise body without a top. This vehicle was no doubt the occasion of much notice, as we find by the town records that it was the only wheeled carriage owned in the place at that time.

Just before his marriage, the diary mentions that Charles Phelps went to Boston to purchase a chaise. Only five of these were owned in town till 1795, and the history of Hadley gives a list of their owners.

A few weeks later, Elizabeth made a visit to

her friend, "Miss Pen," and on her return Charles Phelps takes her home, probably on a pillion, which was the usual custom.

The only comment she makes on this attention is the explanation, "he being a-going to Hatfield."

The Puritan reserve so characteristic of New England, and also, perhaps, natural maiden modesty, prevented any allusions to the subsequent courting. The next time we find the name of her suitor it is as follows: —

"May 13, 1770, Sunday. This day I was published to Mr. Charles Phelps."

The week after, "Rebekah D. came home with me, made me a dark brown ducupe for my wedding-gown, and a light brown taffety for Dolly."

This wedding-gown appears eighteen years afterwards, when we find the note: "Miss Molly W. here to alter my wedding-gown." Again, in 1812, "Hannah altered my wedding-gown."

There is a brief record of "preperations for wedding." Then, June 14th. "A few moments before four o'clock I gave my hand to Charles Phelps. Polly Porter and Dorithy Phelps bridesmaids. We had about twenty couples at wedding. Fryday we had a dinner; the rest were all invited to come in the afternoon."

The merrymaking lasted two days, and the following Sunday she writes: "Many visitors this week."

The bridegroom had a large connection in Northampton, being descended from one of the oldest families in the town. He himself was educated in the profession of the law, and received his commission from Governor Tyrne of New York, in 1771. His contemporaries in legal practice were Joseph Hawley of Northampton, Oliver Partridge of Hatfield, and others. He was a selectman of the town and a justice of the peace.

His ancestors bear an honorable record in the early history of New England. William Phelps came over in the "Mary and John," and represented Dorchester in the General Court the first year of the settlement. He removed with Mr. Warham's church to Windsor, and was one of eight to take charge of the Hartford colony previous to the establishment of the legislature. He is said to have "devoted his whole time to the service of the public as one of its most efficient and valuable officers." He aided in enacting the first laws for the colony in 1639, after the compact of the Connecticut River towns, and was assistant to the governor in the General Assembly. His son Nathaniel moved to Northampton at the planting of that town, and was one of the first deacons of the church. The homestead, which he erected in 1659 was on the ground later occupied by the Gothic seminary for young ladies kept by Miss Dwight. Descendants down to the sixth generation occupied this home for one hundred and seventy-six years. A daughter of Deacon Phelps, Abigail, lived a full century in the town, dying in 1756 at the age of one hundred and two.

The second Nathaniel was the great-grandfather of Charles Phelps. He is mentioned as one of the fathers of the town in 1707. He built a house on the corner of South and Fort streets, which was occupied for five generations during a period of one hundred and twenty-five years.

His wife, Grace Martin, left a strong impress upon the times in which she lived. She is mentioned in early history as "a person of great resolution, and withal a little romantic." This description, which occurs in a number of works of genealogy and biography, always ends: "She has been greatly praised by her descendants."

That she possesssed high spirit, determination, and strength of character, in no common degree, seems undisputed. Whether she had also a strain of imaginative sentiment, a tinge of sensibility approaching sadness, and a contradiction of mood mingled with reserve, which suggested austerity, is open to conjecture. Certain it is that some such traits have been so apparent in her descendants from time to time as to lead to their being traced back to this grandmother whose personality was so marked.

James Savage, in his genealogical researches in Massachusetts, discovered, from what source we know not, the following curious incident in her early life. He says it is " a well-derived tradition as to Grace Martin. Her lover in England was false and married another. She left her native land, came to our country to relatives, the respectable family of Marsh, of Hadley, but in ignorance of their residence, or want of funds, or both, on reaching Boston was in danger of being sold for her passage before relief came from her friends. One version of the story goes further, that she was sold, but it is good enough without this. Her descendants are very numerous, among whom was my distinguished antiquarian friend, Sylvester Judd."

On September 30th there was another wedding in the family, this time the bridesmaid of the former occasion being herself the bride. The entry reads: " Mr. Jonathan Edwards, minister at New Haven, and his two deacons, and Colonel Worcester, came to Hadley. They dined at Esquire Porter's, and then came on to Lawyer Porter's, and Miss Polly gave her hand to Mr. Edwards." This was the same Miss Polly who made one of the party at Cambridge. Her husband was a son of the elder Edwards, and her brother's wife was his sister.

The cousins, who had been dear and intimate friends, are now separated. The young mistress

of Forty Acres begins to find herself engaged
with household matters. Although she has always a hearty interest in her neighbors, and their
joys and sorrows, affairs on the farm are more
frequently referred to. During the early years
of her mother's widowhood, the superintendence
was placed in the hands of a competent man.
Shortly before their marriage, Mr. Phelps took
charge, establishing himself, after the wedding,
on his wife's property. He applied himself at
once to develop its resources and enlarge its
boundaries. Nearly the whole of Mt. Warner
was added to the farm. Part of it was cultivated,
part was used for sheep pasture, and a good deal
more, including Pleasant Hill, was kept as woodlot. This beautiful upland, somewhat like a Swiss
alp in the cleared portions, has always seemed a
sort of fairyland to the children of the family.
Commanding an extensive view from the rocks
on the summit, sloping down to a peaceful millpond, abounding in nut-trees, blackberry vines,
sweet fern, and mountain laurel, it has been a
favorite haunt from early spring to late autumn.
The same pen, which has recalled so much that
was memorable of his boyhood, thus describes
it: " Mt. Warner entered largely into my early
life. Our supplies of fuel all came from it, and
in those days of open fireplaces it was a winter's
work to provide for those voracious consumers of
wood. Then the pastures were there, and every

few days the cattle must be salted. The oxen must be driven to and fro, sometimes the cows, and, in the heat of the season, two or three of us must go on Sunday morning two miles to bring home the horses to go to church. If I remember rightly, the horses disliked being caught as much as some of the boys did going to meeting.

Then there was the washing of the sheep some fine morning in June. This was rare sport, but one who has read Cowper's or perhaps Thompson's description of a sheep-washing would hardly dare attempt anything in the same line. The sheep-shearing, which followed a few days after the washing, had its interest, too, especially for the younger portions of the family. The sheep were driven home and confined in a stable; the barn floor was nicely swept. Then the poor animal, trembling with fright, was brought out and made to assume an awkward sitting posture, where, with its back towards and between the knees of the operator, it resigns itself to its fate. Then the shearer begins his delicate task. Parting the wool under the neck, the nimble shears work their way close to the skin and beneath the matted wool, which soon begins to fall off around the shoulders in fleecy folds, white, soft, yielding to the touch, wonderful in its fresh beauty, as well as in its after uses. After the neck is done the poor sheep is laid on its side; the ringing clip goes relentlessly on, until at last, relieved of its burden, the prisoner leaps forth into native liberty again, but with such diminished size and uncomely proportions as to excite our hearty mirth at the transformation.

Meantime the fleece, which is entire in one piece, is carefully rolled up and tied together to be sent to the carding-mill or sold.

When I was a boy, my father used to raise large fields of rye on Mt. Warner. The preparation of the fields must have cost a great deal of work, but it required stronger hands than mine to turn the furrows on those sidehills and manage the team. When it came to harvesting, I was of more consequence. I could carry the water for the men, and help throw the sheaves together for carting. This water-carrying, by the way, was no light thing.

We used to have a great turn-out of reapers, with their flashing sickles sweeping up the hill, the water coming from a spring at the bottom. I used to think the men drank a most unreasonable quantity.

The rye-harvest was quite an event in the work of the season. I can remember several occasions when the old English custom of shouting the 'Harvest home' was observed.

Another thing must not be forgotten in this connection, and that is the annual apple-gathering. We had enough to do of that at home, and more, but the apple-gathering at Mt. Warner was another thing.

There was the early rising, to lengthen the shortening days; the busy preparation of bags, baskets, vehicles, and provisions; the merry company, for all went that could be spared; the long ride up and back; the dinner by the spring, so much better than at home. The apples, the once famous 'Scott's Sweet,' were sorted, the best being saved for winter apple-sauce, and the poorer ones going into cider.

These Mt. Warner excursions and industries brought us a good deal of hard work, but they had their compensations and enjoyments, as have most of our labors in after life if we look at them the right way.

There was the change of scene: life and labor on Mt. Warner, and life and labor down on the river meadows, were two different things. It may not be easy to define the difference, but it was positive, nevertheless; and as we all like change, this may have contributed to make what might otherwise have seemed hard enjoyable.

Besides this, the view from these pasture lots is one of exceptional beauty. Across the fertile meadows Sugar Loaf and Toby stand out boldly in the north, while between them issues the river, which from this point follows a straight course for several miles until near North Hadley village, when it bears away westward, and, returning again, makes one of those bows of which it is so fond, and at the same time incloses, on three sides, what were known in those days as 'School Meadows.'

This side or eastward of the meadows was the village, and between that and the hillside where our work lay, and which sloped down to its very edge, was the millpond, long and irregular in shape, but not without a certain beauty of its own, which water almost always has.

We were within sound of the village life, and in August, when the ground was being prepared for sowing, the flails of the threshers would beat time all day to the musical drone of the mill.

But in the days of which I am writing, a large part of Mt. Warner was covered with wood, — I will not say forest, for that would imply, perhaps, a larger area than existed, but to my mind they were forests, and the solitudes were immense. There was an air of mystery about them. I could not compass or know them as I did the open fields.

And yet they were fascinating. I would not dare explore their depths alone, for fear of being lost, but, with one who knew them, a plunge from sunlight, song, and flowers into their overhanging shadows, with nothing to break the silence but the distant trill of some solitary wood-thrush, was a strange, awe-inspiring, and, but for the guide at my side, rather a fearful experience, but with one who knew the way exhilarating, a sort of tonic.

What a type it was of some of the after experiences of our lives! Only, in these later ones, it was a deeper life that entered the solitudes. The shadows were darker, the chill more palpable, the thickets more impenetrable, and the silence absolute; no, not that, but only less, because the kind, wise Friend who held us by the hand reassured and led us out again with more tender recollections, with larger lives, and with higher hopes, than we ever knew before.

It was from the woods that we used to get our supplies of birch, — not for our backs, — of winter-green and sassafras, and we used to skirt the edges of this unknown land to secure the necessaries of a boy's inventory of goods and chattels.

But it was the nutting that gave its peculiar charm to the woods. Chestnutting, especially, was the autumn pastime. As early as July, we watched for the long plume-like blossoms, to know if the fruit were likely to be abundant. We welcomed the frosts because they would open the burrs, and, later in the season, the showers of wind and rain were our helpers to beat off the precious burden and lay it at our feet.

Those were hours of high hope and bold adventure, when, some fine morning in October, after a storm, a party of us would start off on one of these nutting expeditions. Numbers gave us daring: the wooded shades were not so dark as in the summer, for the falling leaves let in more light, and we should meet other companies on our way. The bracing air, the pungent odor of the forest known only at this season, no doubt the very exercise of this faculty of search for something we might call our own, all contributed to give a zest to these excursions, which is known only to youth and inexperience.

Then the sense of beauty was constantly stimulated and gratified. I beg you do not laugh at me for expatiating on the beauty of chestnut burrs; but they are like some unlovable people who never open and show their beauty and sweetness until just before they drop into their graves. It is something so with these chestnut burrs and their contents; woe to the boy who steps on one of them barefooted! but show me one whose eyes will not glisten with delight at the sight of one of these freshly fallen prickly globes, full-packed with meat, and opened just enough to show the white satin lining in which sleep these beauties of the wood, and I will confess that we live in a degenerate age.

The color of the chestnut, you know, is a synonym for the richest brown, and the silken scarf which covers the neck is as soft as the eider's down. I think there is nothing that can give us a more impressive sense of the inherent love of beauty that dwells in the divine nature than these chance specimens, as I may almost call them, — the lining of a chestnut-burr, which the weather will spoil in a few hours; or the frost etchings upon a window, so exquisite sometimes in their outline, and yet which a breath will dissolve.

Mt. Warner has no caves or other natural curiosities, that I know of, excepting two large boulders, lying, one in the pasture, and the other in the wood, near the top of the mountain. The latter went by the name of 'John's Rock,' because, as the family tradition said, my grandfather's gardener, a Scotchman, used to visit it on Sundays and take his naps there. The curiosity about those boulders is that they are of a different formation from the surrounding rock, and evidently came from Toby or Sugar Loaf, which I think are of volcanic origin."

The following allusion to Mt. Warner is found in the diary: —

"In the afternoon, my husband carried me up to our mountain farm; walked through much of it; saw a fine prospect of wheat. Oh that it might come to maturity and we enjoy it! I am almost purposed to look around and see how many blessings we have. O God, give one blessing more, even the best!"

The expressions of humble and earnest piety which characterize the private heart-searchings and the home chronicle of Elizabeth's life are frequent. They are sometimes clothed in the quaint language of the time, but are uniformly unaffected and sincere. On her birthday, November 20, 1768, she writes:—

"Satterday. This day one-and-twenty years of age. As I grow in years may I grow in Grace and may the time past of my life more than suffice to me to have wrought the will of the Flesh."

Soon after her marriage she receives from a friend whom she visited an admonition on "the vanity of great appearance; may it be a warning to me never to value myself for grandeur."

After the children came, we find the following tender gratitude:—

"This day, after meeting, our boys came home, told us the wolves had destroyed a number of our sheep and lambs. But, thanks be to God, 't is not our house lambs."

In the church, special thanksgivings and fasts were frequent.

"June 9th, Sunday. This day there was thanks returned to Almighty God for his mercy in not suffering the hurricane, which was at Mountain Gate the night before, to tear them quite to pieces, though it did considerable mischief."

From the reports of the sermons, the favorite theme seems to have been the terrors of judgment. Great efforts were made to alarm the impenitent. The guilty were openly rebuked from the pulpit, and backsliders held up to condemnation.

September 18, 1768, Mr. Hopkins preached two rousing sermons, "reproached all equally, but especially the sin of lying," two persons he had reference to being present in the congregation.

There was, in those days, open concern about personal security in spiritual matters.

They met for prayer at a private house for one "who seems to be in a despairing way." Mental clouding-over almost invariably took this form.

"A meeting was called on Lawyer Porter's account, who continues to be in distress for his soul."

The Puritan conscience was always awake to the sense of direct accountability to its Maker. When the future state of the wicked and the certainty of retribution were depicted in the realistic style common to New England pulpits in the last century, it is no wonder that the effect on sensitive natures was sometimes overwhelming.

If, however, gloom and despair were accompaniments of the religion of those days, there is no doubt that Christian people were, like the Hebrews, sustained by an unshaken confidence in the overruling of Divine Providence. Both loyalty to law itself and to a great Law-giver were strengthened by the large share given in places of worship to matters of public moment. Fasts were held at all times of serious anxiety, sermons preached on questions of common weal, prayers and thanksgivings were offered.

A heavy cloud of disturbance was now gathering, under whose shadow all the patriotism, resolution, and devout faith of the colonists would be called forth.

Only two years after the marriage of Charles Phelps, the town of Hadley took public action on a matter of wider interest than its own local affairs.

Frequent instances had already occurred of oppression by the officials of the crown, and remonstrance had been made against injustice by the people of the provinces.

The Hadley freemen maintained, like the Massachusetts Assembly, that the king to whom allegiance was sworn should be the sole umpire between them and the British Parliament.

They voted at town meeting, in 1772, "that our grievances be made known to His Majesty."

In August, 1774, there is threatening of war. The diary says: "Just at night my husband came home from town with terrible news that the army of forces, which are stationed in Boston, had begun to fight, and were coming out into the Country spreading destruction wherever they came. Distressing night. But the Lord is our Trust."

"November 13, 1774. Publick affairs are at present very dark."

Fast days are now frequently referred to, sometimes local, at other times appointed by the Provincial Congress.

"April 23, 1775. In the afternoon my Husband set out for Brookfield as a post, to hear what News, for last Wednesday the Troops and our men had a Battle, numbers lost on both sides, but it seems as if we were most favored. O most gracious Lord, save from the spilling of human Blood, pray save Thy people, our Eyes are unto Thee."

"June 25, 1775. News has come this week from our Army at Cambridge, and round about there, that they had a battle last week Satterday, about fifty killed, some wounded, some taken. It is said, that many more of the Regulars are killed than of the provincials; they have taken ground from our men: the event is thine, most Gracious God; we are ready to view it as a frowning providence, but O our God, our Fathers trusted in thee, and were not ashamed; we desire to come out of ourselves, to renounce our own strength. The Race is not to the swift nor the Battle to the strong, salvation is the Lord's; we are a distressed people, extremely dry we are here and there was a frost last Tuesday night which has cut down almost all the corn hereabouts, the most severe one I suppose ever known at this season of the year. God is righteous; O may I learn to rejoice in the Lord (whatever distress) and joy in the God of my salvation."

"July 20, 1775. A Universal fast recommended by the Continental Congress to all the

English Inhabitants of this vast and extensive Continent."

"August 13. Friday went down to Mr. Thomas Smith's to get Lydia to show me how to make a pair of breeches, for the soldiers' people are sent to find 'em clothes."

"August 20. A number of prisoners went thro' this town to Northampton gail taken from the Regulars."

"February 25, 1776. My husband set out for Cambridge; his team Goodrich went away with loaded with flour."

"March 3. Our men this day set out for Quebeck, a number of them came and presented themselves in the broad alley. Mr. Hopkins rose and told their desire of the prayers of the people, then they bowed and went off. Bless 'em, pray Father bless 'em."

"March 19. This day the Regulars left Boston, which they have held as their Garrison this year. Glory to God."

"May 11. Friday a Continental Fast; a mighty force it is said is coming against this land. O our God, they can have no might nor power against us except it be given them from above. In the name of the Lord of Hosts, the God of the Armies of Israel, may we lift up our banners."

"July 14. Mr. Lyman preached a sermon to the men that have enlisted to go to the relief of our Northern Army."

"July 6, 1777. Very bad news this week; our forts at Ticonderoga given up to our enemies hand. God is righteous."

"July 13th. Great part of the militia went to the Northward last week."

"August 17, 1777, Sunday. Awakened this morning about four o'clock with the ringing of Hatfield Bell; soon heard it was an alarm from the Westward; many men set out to go; none of our family at meeting but John the Regular Captive, and Jacob (he was bound here a year ago) but I can't find where the text was, all seems to be confusion."

This is the only Sunday in a period of forty-seven years, except in sickness, when the text of the sermon is not carefully entered.

"August 21, 1777. The event of the late alarm was that the enemy sent out a party to come and destroy the outposts, but the people rose, and the Lord ordered it that they met with a great defeat; drove 'em back to a wood. Not unto us, not unto us, but to the Lord, be the glory thou had begun to save, our eyes, pray Father, are unto Thee, we desire to come and wait for deliverance at thy hand and in thy way and time."

"September 20th. Another alarm. O Lord, I tremble."

"October 19th. Dined at Col. Porter's. He came just before two, confirmed the good news of Burgoyne's having surrendered up his whole army Oh wonderful, wonderful, words can't express our adoration and praise Glory and Power and Might be given to the Lord Almighty! All to Thee! All to Thee! Utterly unworthy we! the Lord has done it; pray, Father, perfect this begun goodness. Oh that all may see the hand of God. I desire to fall down in astonishment!"

The retreat of Burgoyne's army was through Hadley, then on the direct road from Albany to Boston. Of their march this record is made:—

"October 26, 1777. Our whole family Left home to see the Regulars pass, but only the babe and me."

Esquire Porter, so often referred to, was a colonel in the Revolutionary War, and commanded troops in the campaign against Burgoyne. When his distinguished adversary passed through Hadley after his surrender, Colonel Porter invited him to stay at his house, while the soldiers encamped in the meadow. The courtesy was so generously appreciated by the British officer that he left behind his sword as a recognition of the hospitality extended to him. This memento, which is of beautiful workmanship, is treasured among the descendants to the present time.

In an earlier generation, before such relics became of value, it lay forgotten, and was at last discovered by the great-granddaughters, who now preserve it, hidden in a chest between piles of blankets.

On one of his visits at home during the Revolution, Colonel Porter brought with him a Scotchman, a prisoner of war. He entered the service of Charles Phelps, and was the "Captive" previously referred to. By that name he was known for some time, but was remembered in later years as John Morrison, the gardener.

"This was his especial business in the summer season, and from what I have heard he must have been bred to the employment. He was a relic of the British army of the Revolution, and chose to remain in this country after the war.

I doubt if at that time there was a farmer in the three counties who kept a professional gardener, that is, one whose exclusive business was ornamental gardening. I never knew the garden in its prime, but our mother often spoke of its beauties, and I can remember how sad it made her feel to have those sacred precincts invaded by the unfeeling plough and boorish oxen, that would as soon tread upon the fairest flower as upon a thistle. I imagine old John's indignation could hardly have found words to express itself, vehement as he sometimes was in his speech, could he have seen the profanation. Why, there were few precious hands good enough even to turn the sacred soil; and as to flowers, woe to the luckless one outside the household who should dare to brave his wrath by even touching one of his floral treasures.

THE HOUSE, FROM THE GARDEN

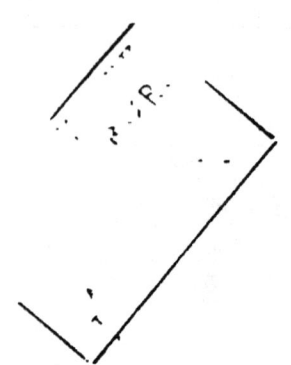

And yet he had the Scotch humor. He cultivated the sensitive plant, very rare in those days. He would amuse himself sometimes by getting one unacquainted with its peculiarities to touch it, and then witness the fright and sudden collapse. I used to hear many of his *bons mots*, but remember only one. When any nice dish was being discussed, the foundation of which was ordinary material, he used to say : ' You can make my old boots good by putting enough butter on them.' "

Another captive, a Hessian, was brought from the wars. After he settled permanently on the farm, he probably sent for his wife, for it is recorded that they lived for years in a little hut at the foot of Pleasant Hill. An old German Psalm Book in the family library must have belonged to them. They evidently retained the customs of their native land, foreign to Puritan New England. Mrs. Phelps mentions in the diary that she and her husband took supper one Christmas Eve with " Mary and Andries," perhaps at that time the only celebration of the occasion in the country round. An old letter describes the pitiful condition of the poor woman, alone in a strange land, when her husband died.

Again and again she wailed, " Mein Andries, mein Andries, what shall I now doon ? "

She was tenderly cared for, taken into the large house, and provided with a home during the remainder of her life. It is evident that it was a great trial to a Yankee housekeeper to admit into her spotless dwelling one whose peasant habits were somewhat offensive. Mrs. Phelps, however, rebukes herself for the struggle, and with characteristic cheerfulness assumes the burden. The difficulty was increased, as she says, for " she can understand so little what we say, and we so poorly understand her."

There is a record in the diary of prayers offered in the village meeting during the anxious time of Andries' sickness, and of the solicitude with which he was nursed.

Those were not the days of institutions to which all classes of sufferers could be relegated, — of organized relief societies, bureaus, and refuges. A family like that of Charles and Elizabeth Phelps provided out of their own means for those fellow-creatures living in direct relation to them, and for the wider circle of neighbors who were in trouble or want.

Good sense and a broad spirit of charity alike taught them to make allowance for the moral infirmities consequent upon dependence, and for the inherent weakness of human nature.

One of those cases peculiarly difficult to deal with, and often so discouraging as to be abandoned, was that of a young woman whom Mrs. Phelps befriended and brought up. For years her letters are full of anxious care for " Mitty."

Again and again she took the girl back, under circumstances which must have made her almost hopeless. Still she continued to strengthen and stimulate the feeble nature, making all excuses possible for that restlessness and impatience of control natural to youth. In the end, after several lapses, Mitty made a respectable marriage and lived to old age, honored by her children and grandchildren, and giving faithful service in the family to whose head she owed so much.

Of the other hired help, Mrs. Phelps was always most considerate. She praised them for their faithfulness, was solicitous for their welfare, and took unwearied pains in the training of the young.

In later years her letters to her daughter, full of domestic details, have no complaints of the servants, but frequent allusions to them, satisfaction with their care in her absence, messages to them, interest in their affairs. For some time after her marriage, there were several African slaves in the household, who are often mentioned. In 1772 she writes: "Our Peg, who has Lived with us near eighteen years, of her own choice left her children and was sold to one Capt. Fay with a negro man from this town, for the sake of being his wife."

In 1782 notice is taken of a woman who has left, "gone off free."

A young slave girl was tenderly cared for during a lingering decline, and in meeting "Prayers were offered for our Phyllis being very Low." In the extreme cold weather a great chest was made into a warm bed and placed in the large kitchen, and there the poor child died.

Peace was at last restored after the long public disturbances.

"December 30, 1778. Thanksgiving through all the United States of America. Will the Lord be pleased to bless the State of America."

Among the delegates to the Continental Congress in Philadelphia was Charles Phelps, senior, the father of Charles, by whose wife frequent mention is made of him in the pages of her diary.

This singular man was endowed in a large degree with that mixture of romance and resolution which Grace Martin bequeathed to her descendants. The history of his life is that of one whose ideal of action was so high, and his adherence to it so unflinching, that all other considerations were set at nought.

His birthplace and early home were in Northampton, where he married Dorothy Root, "a lady of spirit and character." Several years before the marriage of his son Charles, he disposed of his property in Hadley, where he had been residing, and took up land grants on the western side of the Connecticut River, beyond the boundary of Massachusetts. In this country, which was then a wilderness, he established himself with his family.

His grandson, John Phelps, has written out an interesting narrative connected with those days. He says: "In the township of New Marlboro', at the foot of the Green Mountains, with no neighbors but beasts of prey, they built their cabins to shield them against that most inclement climate.

Here they commenced felling the formidable forests around them. It was no holiday sport, this. Nor had they any reasonable prospect of wealth to incite them. Nor was it to enjoy freedom of conscience that they sacrificed every hope of enjoyment for an age at least; because, at that very moment, the Southern Colonies, with a more genial climate and generous soil, lay equally open to their enterprise. Nations are founded as Providence orders. Moved by a severe and fearless impulse, the iron men and women that planted themselves among the rocks and evergreen wildernesses of New England had for an immediate object, no doubt, a home; but theirs was a higher ministry, unknown to them, that they were performing. They were planting a nursery for the propagation of nations, to be transplanted in due time to the vast and fertile valleys of 'The West.'

Sixteen years of labor, toil, and hardship found them in the midst of a large clearing; fields of grass and grain around them; sheep, cattle, and horses in their pastures, and pigs and poultry in their yards, — the enjoyment of which, however, was yet disputed by bears, wolves, catamounts, and other vermin of the forest. At length, however, other inhabitants had begun to settle on 'The Grants,' and other clearings had begun to dot the hillsides and forests. Grinding and saw mills had been erected."

In this spot, still remote from the world, Charles Phelps conceived the high purpose of building and endowing a college. Although it never reached completion, the imagination of its projector, living on the hilltops in a dream of his own creation, seems to have endowed it with a glow of romance.

The following quaint account shows what an impression was made through him on the mind of his second wife, and the circumstances of their marriage: —

"My grandmother Phelps died in 1775. The family in this event suffered a great loss, which, as far as my grandfather was concerned, he repaired a few months after by marrying another wife, one of the sweetest and most amiable of women, Mrs. Anstis Eustis Kneeland, a fair and handsome widow of thirty, after a romantic courtship of one day, he being about sixty years of age. This lady belonged to the ancient and honorable family of Eustis in Boston; was the widow of a Mr. Kneeland, a respectable printer of that place, who had died a year or two before.

The morning after the wedding it was announced in a morning paper. As there is something even in this notice that gives some idea of the character of the gentleman, I subjoin it: 'Married, by the Rev. Mr. ——, according to the forms of the venerable Church of England, the Honorable Charles Phelps, late one of his Majesty's Justices of the Common Pleas, *a gentleman of uncommon politeness*, to the interesting and accomplished Mrs. Anstis Eustis Kneeland, relict of Mr. Kneeland, late of Boston, printer, after a romantic Courtship of 24 hours.'

It was understood in the family that it was the aunt of Mrs. Kneeland, Mrs. Eustis, also a widow lady, much nearer the age of my grandfather, that he was in pursuit of for a wife. His call at her elegant mansion was to declare this his intention. This princess of a lady declined the honor intended her, but politely informed him that she had a niece visiting with her, also a widow, to whom an offer of this kind might be more agreeable; and she thereupon introduced her. The young lady, all covered with blushes, and trembling with apprehension, received the salutation of an old gentleman, large and corpulent, six feet three inches in the clear, in full bottom wig, frizzed and powdered in the most approved style, either for the judicial bench or ladies' drawing-room.

The announcement of the question immediately followed. The lady turned pale. Her delicacy was shocked. With overpowered sensations she begged to withdraw a moment. Her aunt also gently obtained leave of absence and followed. After a short consideration the ladies both returned. 'Judge Phelps,' remarked the elder lady, 'we are taken by surprise. The subject is deeply important. My niece, although favorably impressed, asks time to consider. She presumes upon your delicacy, and is assured that if it at all corresponds with your gallantry, you will indulge her a short space for reflection, say one week, after which, if you will honor us with a call, my niece — we, I mean — will be better prepared.'

'Preparation! Dearest madam, do me the favor to commit all preparation to my care. I am so happy in this respect that I have already hinted to a dear friend of mine, a Presbyterian minister of the Kirk of Scotland (to which Evangelical communion I have no doubt you conform), that I may have need.'

'Not on account of the marriage of my niece, sir! By a Presbyterian! That will never do, never, sir!'

Alas, how liable are the most eager hopes and expectations to receive a chill! In the way of his own cherished profession, the gentleman was brought up with a special demurrer here, and that by a lady.

With the astute eye of a lawyer, however, he perceived that the lady had committed a departure from the original issue, which was matter of substance, — to wit: marry now or not marry at all, — and had closed upon a new issue, and that, too, of a mere Presbyterian form, of no substance at all. He therefore adroitly proposed, in the most eloquent and polite terms, to the ladies, and in a manner most condescending, that on reflection he cheerfully yielded in matter of form to their superior propriety and taste, and would be married in any church they might choose on the morrow morning, so that in the afternoon they might set out on their journey to his seat in 'The Grants.'

The ladies, a little surprised, but on the whole gratified, at this easy way of shoving off a difficulty, and feeling not a little proud of their triumph over the Presbyterian; the first concession being yielded to the lady argued well for her future supremacy. The definitive arrangement was settled accordingly; and on the morrow, the skillful diplomatist and gratified groom, with his happy and admiring bride, was on his way to Vermont.

This lady, now a bride, possessed one master sentiment: it was love. This taught her the most pleasant duty of being subject to her adored husband in all things. It also covered all her husband's deficiencies and faults, and there was great need. Having no sense of comfort himself, he provided none for others.

Therefore, when his lady arrived at her new home, she found it to be a sort of castle built of hewed logs, standing in a bleak open field, recently partly cleared, stumps, logs, and other vestiges of rude creation surrounding it; unfinished at the time and never afterwards finished.

The original design of the building was large and magnificent. In the basement were mills, worked by hand or horse-power, for grinding corn. On the first floor was a spacious hall, with folding doors at either end, through which the north winds were wont to sweep at pleasure. In this hall, also, was the staircase.

Entering this hall from the south, on your left you entered the grand parlor; next was a spare sleeping-room; and lastly, on the extreme end, was his honor's chosen library, composed of the best authors of the day, on divinity, law, physics, belles-lettres, etc., divinity and law occupying by far the heavier shelves. On the right side of the hall were his honor's dining hall, cook room, sleeping room, and two bedrooms as convenient appendages. The two upper stories were designed as rooms for a college establishment, recitation rooms, lecture rooms, and dormitories for young gentlemen students.

By his honor's will, executed a few days before his death, this whole college establishment was solemnly dedicated and set apart for an institution of learning, in perpetuity, and endowed with many ten thousand acres of his Draper and Somerset estates. Young Moses Porter Phelps, son of Charles Phelps, Esq., of Old Hadley, then a student in Cambridge College, was duly appointed first president thereof, with power, for the time being, over the whole building, domestic as well as scientific and literary, — over the whole library, philosophical apparatus, chemical, geometrical, and mathematical instruments. Provided always, that when he arrived at suitable years, became duly qualified, showed genius for government, had scientific and literary abilities; was deeply imbued with religion, according to the doctrines of the Kirk of Scotland; had taken to himself a sober, discreet, and exemplary wife, of the same religious views and doctrines; and provided, also, that he would reside in the same college building and make it his home.

From this glowing description, given in a solemn matter-of-fact paper, we may judge what was the description of it given to his Boston bride before she saw it. The gentleman certainly was making unauthorized drafts upon his imagination; or rather he was describing what his house and college might be, rather than what it was.

There were no chimneys, no glass windows, no recitation rooms, no dormitories, no floors. The upper stories were always used for hay-lofts. It was to such a house as this, with all its future destinies in prospect, that the Boston lady was introduced, and of which she became mistress.

One of the first visible objects, after my mother and perhaps my father, that I remember to have set my young admiring eyes upon, was this Boston lady, whom, in rude and rustic familiarity, we used to call 'Granny.' Methinks I see her now, of a fine summer's afternoon or evening, dressed to see her little Johnny, some four years of age, the only quality she expected, unless, upon an evening of uncommon leisure, when my lively-spirited mother might accompany me. There she sits, clad in rich changeable silks, gold watch with heavy establishment in her girdle; a double chain of gold, connected in front with a large precious stone locket set in gold, around her delicately turned neck; golden bracelets around her wrists.

There she sits, that Boston lady of the olden time. Methinks I see her now, and hear, too, that soft and gentle 'ahem,' as if to prepare her voice for the sweetest and tenderest welcome; and feel, too, those glowing, hearty kisses. I sit upon her knee; I hear her charming stories; I say my prayer; I receive my cake, with her parting kiss and blessing, and run home a happier and better boy.

This lady was left comfortably off by my grandfather. For two or three years after his death she kept up the family mansion, the old college edifice. She kept a fine table, which she knew how to set forth in excellent style, so as to show her taste and thrift to the best advantage. She often indulged in, to her, the great luxury of giving a dinner, at which I had sometimes the honor of being a guest. Her person, address, style of living, and rich conversational powers obtained for her many admirers. But she gloried in my grandfather, and never tired in setting forth his worth. In this duty nature, admiration, and love all combined, for he possessed a noble, commanding person.

A frame six feet three inches in height, erect, ample, bony, gave full scope to a body inclining to be corpulent to favorably develop itself. Light gray, lustrous eyes, finely set beneath ample, capacious brows, gave to a high, squarely turned forehead a sense both of firmness and power.

His dress on ordinary, every-day occasions was mean, badly attended to, and slovenly. But when dressed for public occasions, nothing could be more magnificent, fashionable, or in better taste. The finest linen, frilled at wrist and bosom with the most costly cambrics; golden buckles to his stock, costly gems for buttons to his wristbands; deep blue broadcloth coat of the finest and firmest material; buff vest and smallclothes silk stockings, with shoes or boots to fit. And then the wig, — that ample, full-bottomed, full-powdered wig, of the style of Louis XIV., or George III.; to which add the brilliant on his finger, and the rings in his ears, the whole being surmounted with the tasteful chapeau-de-bras, with buttons of gold."

The diary mentions the death of the first wife of Charles Phelps, Sen., as occurring September 13, 1777.

In that year there were frequent visits of the old gentleman. In May, 1778, he was on his way to Boston.

"June. Father came, and a woman who he is going to take up to Marlborough to spin and weave, one widow."

"December 29. Father Phelps came here and brought a wife (she was the widow Kneeland, of Boston)."

There is a letter still preserved written by Charles Phelps, at the time his son Solomon, afterwards a graduate of Harvard, was in college: —

"To the Reverend and Honorable Edward Holyoke Esqr., President of Harvard College, and the ever respectable tutors of the same.

After compliments paid you upon a grateful remembrance of the favor and respect you have shown me, I earnestly desire the favor of permitting my son at college to return home with his brother before Thanksgiving, with whom I have sent a horse for him to ride up, if you, gentlemen, will permit him to do so; confidently relying upon it that, if I could with conveniency suggest the reasons, my desire would not be denied.

I am gentlemen, with great respect,
Your very humble and much obliged servant,
at command, CHARLES PHELPS.

HADLEY, *Nov.* 26, A. D. 1761."

Soon after the Revolutionary War, Charles Phelps, Sen., became engaged in a hot contention concerning the jurisdiction over the towns of New Marlboro' and others in Cumberland County, part of what was originally known as "The New Hampshire Grants." This territory, having organized under the laws of the State of New York, resisted the authority of the newly formed State of Vermont, and remained firm in its allegiance to New York. By the recommendation of Congress, each district was to maintain its own constitution and laws. Under this arrangement Charles Phelps received the appointment of chief justice, and his son Timothy that of high sheriff.

When disputes began to arise, and Vermont enforced her demand for taxes in the disaffected towns, Mr. Phelps traveled to Philadelphia to maintain his claim before Congress. Its decision was that the governor of New York State should direct its loyal subjects in Cumberland County to resist the impositions of the State of Vermont. To those who supported this ruling, the encroachments of Vermont, in annexing portions of New Hampshire and New York, seemed usurping and dangerous. New York State pledged civil and military support in the contest. The Cumberland County militia, loyal to New York, organized and overcame the Vermont constables and sheriff. At this point, however, General Ethan Allen crossed the mountains with his troops and quelled the disturbance.

The insurgents were tried, and condemned to banishment.

Charles Phelps was still in Philadelphia trying to obtain redress. His property had been confiscated, and history represents him at this time in distress from poverty and exile, but determined to win his cause if possible. To him a principle was involved which required the sacrifice of every personal consideration.

His son Timothy was among those ordered to leave the State. Being, however, as fully convinced as his father of the justice of their cause, and believing that it would finally triumph, he quietly returned to his home and settled down on the farm. His son thus describes the attitude he assumed: —

"The scenes that were enacted in these border feuds were amusing, and at this day would be ludicrous; the reason for which was, that the combatants were neighbors acting under disputed authorities, neither of which felt entirely confident that it would be justified in the end. The constables of Windham County, with their assistants, would come with their warrants for taxes; my father, as Sheriff of Cumberland County, would read to them the riot act, whereupon the affrighted constables would retire for fresh instructions. But after the decree of banishment, the riot act in the mouth of my father seemed to have lost its effect. An occasion soon presented itself which required decisive measures.

My father one morning, pitchfork in hand, was feeding his oxen, preparatory to his day's occupation, when a constable with his suite appeared, and made proclamation that he distrained the oxen for taxes, and was proceeding to drive them off for that purpose. My father placed himself before the oxen with his pitchfork, and ordered the constable to desist, at his peril.

The constable not obeying, but persisting in driving the cattle off, my father effectually rescued them by knocking down the constable for dead with the fork; upon which the assistants fled, and my father went about his business as usual; soon, however, to be disturbed and routed by another Green Mountain army under another Gen. Allen."

Mrs. Timothy Phelps was quite equal to her husband in the resolution she displayed. On the occasion of one of these raids of General Ira Allen in search of her husband, she was engaged with her servants at the household washing in Mill River. "She had scarcely got well into the suds, when she saw splashing into the ford-way more than forty armed men, all mounted, with their drawn swords waving and glittering in the sunbeams; and to her great surprise and regret, she saw this armed body of enemies piloted and conducted by her old friend and neighbor, Col. W. As soon as they approached the place where she was stationed, with a spirit more undaunted than that of any hero, because with the spirit of a betrayed and injured woman, she stepped forward and said: 'Col. W., you grieve and amaze me. I had not expected meanness and treachery like this in a friend like you.' Saying this, and not waiting for an apology which W. was attempting to stammer out, she took me by the hand, and, ordering her maid to run, she proceeded quick step for the house, not exactly in sight, but only some quarter of a mile distant. The little tow-headed almshouse boy, having instinctively snuffed the object of this warlike movement, had instantly and unnoticed taken himself off, and under cover of a large grove of poplars, with almost greyhound speed, had given notice to my father of the near approach of the enemy.

The armed force in the mean time had arrived,

and after wheeling, in great military display, two or three times around the house, dismounted, forced the door, and went in; my mother, with her child in her hand, following in short and quick order into the house, of which she no sooner gained possession than a volley of before-unheard-of eloquence, commencing 'Cowardly miscreants,' assailed their ears. Evidently they soon began to feel abashed and distressed. Being gentlemen, generous and gallant, they seemed perplexed how to act in so novel an affair. They demanded to be shown my father. She denied and defied them; telling them to go to Col. W., and not come to her, a woman and a wife, to aid them in their oppression, tyranny, and robbery; all this while following them up, armed with large kitchen fire-shovel; warning them, in the most firm though stormy and indignant manner, ' to leave the house, upon the peril of having their brains laid open; mean, contemptible, cowardly banditti as they were. Draw your poltroon swords upon a woman and her infants, will you? brave heroes as you are. Use them if you dare. A day of awful reckoning is at hand for you, my worthies.'

It was distressing for me to see, not my mother indeed, but those whom she was so hotly pursuing, though annoyed by me all the while at her apron strings.

At one time one might see them dodging into

a corner, as if to escape her blows; at another endeavoring to provoke a laugh by some affected attempt at wit. All would not do. They were men who had learned humanity in a better school than that in which they found themselves engaged, and had not been taught to war on defenseless woman, or ruthlessly break the doors of her private chambers.

After laughing themselves, and at length my mother also, into a fit of good feeling, they took her naked word that my father was not in the house, which was true; and after suitable apologies, and kind wishes for the return of mutual friendship and confidences, with profound courtesy and politeness they departed.

But it was no part of my father's character to shun the face of a fellow-mortal, and the cavalcade was scarcely out of sight before he reappeared in the midst of his family. But he was allowed to remain only a few days. A deputy sheriff was sent at the head of some eight or ten assistants, and, suddenly entering our house early in the morning, seized and imprisoned my father. The direct route to the jail lay through the town of Brattleborough. While the sheriff was passing with his prisoner, a large collection of Yorkers, assembled for raising a building in that town, sprang from the frame, handspikes in hand, rescued my father, who was their sheriff, and sent the Vermont sheriff with his posse home, to try his luck again.

My father thereupon was immediately provided with a horse and all necessary accommodations, together with a strong guard, to conduct him beyond the line of Vermont into Massachusetts, which done he pursued his way to the residence of Charles Phelps, his brother, in Hadley.

An increased force immediately set about a pursuit and recapture; came in the dead of night, pell-mell, upon my uncle's residence, and thundered at his doors. My uncle, springing from his bed and calling for his servants and his arms, rushed to the door. The sheriff and his men were already in. A struggle ensued. My uncle was overpowered and floored, and they were proceeding to bind him, when Mrs. Phelps, my uncle's wife, claimed him for her husband. By this time my father appeared, and was secured and hurried off towards Vermont. No time was lost on the other side. My uncle flew to the High Sheriff of Hampshire County (his wife's cousin, Col. Porter) with a hue and cry.

The posse was forthwith rallied, together with the local militia, which happened at that time to be commanded by my uncle.

All being well-mounted, and armed to the teeth, a hot pursuit commenced. The Vermonters were overtaken at Bloody Brook, in Deerfield, at about eight o'clock in the morning, where they had dismounted to refresh horses and men. No time was given to rally, but sword in hand the Hampshire County boys rushed in upon them while at breakfast, and captured every man.

They were all taken back and secured in Northampton jail, the common receptacle at that time for all disorderly birds from Vermont."

Mrs. Charles Phelps thus describes the occurrence: —

"January 19, 1784, Monday. Five men came to take Brother Timothy, they abused my Husband and took Tim. Went off — we had a most dreadful fright but Blessed be God no lives lost — my Husband went to Col. Porter and a number of men pursued 'em, brought 'em back. Tuesday had the court at Northampton. Brother went on to New York."

While these stirring events were occurring under the family roof-tree, the elder Charles continued in Philadelphia, and published there a pamphlet entitled "Vermonters Unmasked," in which he argued conclusively in favor of the New York party. "He did not fail to present to all the States the danger they were in, if the audacious precedent attempted to be established by Vermont of dismembering, as they had lately done, New Hampshire and New York, and annexing to their own already usurped dominion so large territories of independent States, should be allowed."

In response to these representations Congress

passed resolutions restoring all the confiscated property of the insurgents, and rescinding their orders of banishment.

This action was, however, defied and ignored by the State of Vermont. Timothy Phelps, in full confidence of his credentials, clothed with his official dress and emblazoned with the insignia of authority, boldly attempted to read the resolutions of Congress in the presence of the Supreme Court of Vermont. The house was thrown into confusion by the aggressive and determined attitude of the New York sheriff. A scene of tumult ensued, and Phelps was arrested and imprisoned as a traitor and insurgent, with others of his party.

After a winter's suffering in the privation of a common jail, there now seemed no further course open than submission. Yielding to the entreaties of his wife, he gave his allegiance to the authorities of Vermont. This concession gained for him at once the honorable treatment and attentions of his opponents, who could not fail to admire the resolution he had displayed.

His father, Charles Phelps, was steadfast to the last.

"Repudiating all advice, refusing all assistance, disdaining to petition those whose power he resisted and defied, he remained a prisoner of state, in close confinement, long after every reasonable mind had become convinced that Vermont had cleared the way for a triumphal entry into the Federal Union.

A political revolution, which in no case ever goes back, in this case was not likely to be impeded in the slightest degree by any individual suffering it might occasion; but would roll on, with increased momentum and power, to its final consummation, leaving those who had been overthrown, by endeavoring to stop the movement, to recover themselves the best way they could.

This state of things had become apparent to every one but him. He took no measures, nor would he consent that any should be taken, for his deliverance. For this he was ultimately indebted to measures taken by his son, Charles Phelps, Jr., Esq., of Massachusetts, without the knowledge and consent of his father. This gentleman, by a petition to the Governor and Council of Vermont, obtained for him a free and unqualified pardon, with an order for the restitution of such of his estates as then remained in the government to restore. When his prison doors were opened to him, he showed surprise and chagrin rather than joy and satisfaction; and that no future advantage should be taken of him even by inference that he had anywise subjected himself to the authority he opposed, before leaving the prison he gave public notice, 'That he recognized no power in Vermont even to release him; and that he left not by legal authority, but from want of physical power in his enemies to detain him longer.'

With this he returned to his family, and the remainder of his life was spent in preparing documents, facts, and arguments to induce Congress to make good their resolutions of the 5th of December, 1782. He left large masses of well-labored papers prepared to this end.

In his will, executed in 1789, he styles himself Charles Phelps of New Marlborough, in the County of Cumberland, in the State of New York. All he says about Vermont is, 'That its people had got his lands and other estate, and thereby impoverished him.' "

His experience of personal distress, forfeiture of fortune, and disappointment in a hopeless cause seems never to have daunted this determined character. Nothing availed to him in comparison with the justice of his claim. The contention over the New Hampshire Grants, with the excited feeling, and local divisions which it caused, goes to show out of what discordant elements the peace of the nation was effected under the American Constitution. It is fortunate for our country that its founders had neither the hot blood nor the dogged temper of Charles Phelps, but were men endowed with wisdom, moderation, and breadth of view. At the same time the descendants of a patriot, who sacrificed everything for a principle, in which his only personal concern was loss rather than gain, will not disown their birthright, or fail in respect for his character.

The town of New Marlborough still slumbers among the hills, remote as of old from share in the great currents of outside progress. The great University has crumbled into dust. Children and grandchildren who inherited the remains of the large estate have gone out into the world to bear their part in the stirring life of our new civilization. Strangers now till the rocky pastures which surround the family burying place. The retreat of habitation, so deplored in our solitary New England towns, has left this little "God's Acre" far away from the tread of man. The occasional pilgrim, moved to offer a tribute to the rugged character of a forefather, searches with difficulty for the inclosure. He finds it abandoned to the wild and tangled verdure which is the only luxuriance of the granite hills. The old man lies in the stillness and the clear atmosphere of the uplands amid whose inspirations his soul gained its unwavering adherence to truth and right.

In reference to the afore-mentioned events the diary says:—

"1782, September 8. Father Phelps came here, there has been great commotion about a new state, got to bloodshed but none killed yet as we know of. O most mighty God, all are in

THE FAMILY BURIAL-PLACE

thine hands as clay in the hand of the potter, glorify thy name if it may be command peace, be better than our fears but surely we will endeavor to honor God in all situations in Life."

"October 10. Brother Timothy came here in trouble there about the state."

"December 24. Brother Timothy came here again fled from home."

"February 25, 1784. My husband set out for Bennington to get Father out of jail. Saturday eve. got home had success in his business for which I return thanks to God."

"October 21. My husband set out for Vermont to do some business for Father."

The 19th of April, 1781, has always been remembered in New England as a day of uncommon inclemency for that date. In the diary we find "a great storm of hail and snow."

The following year came a sad affliction in the loss of Mrs. Phelps's bridesmaid and cousin.

"1782, July 1. Just at dark Sam. Porter came here and brought the melancholy news of Mrs. Edwards' death said she was drowned watering her Horse went in too far, my dear friend the companion of my childhoood and youth." The next year she says: "June 29, Mrs. Edwards two daughters Polly 10, Jerusha 8. O how dear they are to me for their mother's sake!"

The disturbed condition of the country after the Revolutionary war, and the consequent financial embarrassment, led to the popular uprising known as "Shays' Rebellion." Such serious discord was threatened that Washington wrote to Lincoln in Massachusetts, "Are your people getting mad? Are we to have the goodly fabric, that eight years were spent in raising, pulled down over our heads?" The principal causes of discontent were, the universal indebtedness, and the scarcity of money. Efforts of creditors to collect what was due them were resisted. Among the turbulent and unprincipled of the community, the cry was, "Down with the courts of law, prevent the judges from acting, and hang the lawyers."

A convention met at Hatfield, August 22, 1786, and made out a list of grievances. Fifteen hundred armed men assembled at Northampton the same month, to prevent the session of the Court of Common Pleas. Daniel Shays, a captain in the Revolutionary war, of doubtful reputation, headed the insurgents in Hampshire County. At Springfield a large body collected to prevent the meeting of the Supreme Court.

The difficulties threatened were so grave that the state militia was ordered out, and placed under the command of General Lincoln. On the 20th of January the troops marched to Worcester to protect the courts there. An attempt was now made on the part of the insurgents to gain possession of the United States Arsenal at Springfield. They were dispersed by General Shephard with the loss of several of their men.

Shays retreated to Amherst, whither he was followed by General Lincoln on the 29th, upon whose arrival he took refuge on the Pelham Hills while the militia were quartered at Hadley and Hatfield. On the 30th General Lincoln sent a letter to Shays advising him to surrender, giving a promise that the privates, if they at once laid down their arms, should be recommended for mercy. Shays asked time to petition the General Court, and many letters were sent to General Lincoln begging him to suspend hostilities until a new Legislature should be chosen. He was, however, resolute in demanding, first of all, the disbanding of the troops. Failing this, he prepared his forces for an attack on the party at Pelham. The insurgents started at once on a retreat across the hills to Petersham. Lincoln followed by a hurried night's march. It was midwinter; a north wind arose, the roads were filled with snow. Through large districts no shelter could be obtained, and the whole distance, thirty miles, was traversed between eight o'clock in the evening and nine the next morning. Taken as it was by men unaccustomed to the field, and in the inclemency of the severest month in the year, it was long celebrated among the annals of New England adventure. This rapid movement proved successful. Shays's men had made the journey earlier, before the change in the weather, which occurred after midnight. They were resting, and sleeping off their exertions, when the militia surprised them. One hundred and fifty were captured, and thus the campaign ended without a drop of blood shed among the soldiers of the Commonwealth, who had crossed a wide section of the State, and routed two bodies of armed men.

After some further disturbances in Berkshire County, and the neighboring States where the disaffected had taken refuge, quiet was restored, and after April no alarms occurred.

Such riot and threatening of war near at home were naturally a cause of anxiety at Forty Acres. The diary says: "1786, September 25. Monday my Husband set out for Springfield; publick affairs seem to be in a confused situation many are gone to prevent the sitting of the Court and many are gone to uphold the Court. O Lord bring order out of disorder. Thou canst effect it. We trust in allmighty power."

"Thursday Mr. Phelps returned in safety, no lives lost."

"December 15, Thursday Thanksgiving day. Mr. Hopkins preached no sermon. Col. Porter read an address from the General Court to all the people in this Commonwealth, there has been a great deal of Disturbance of late among the people, how it will terminate God only knows.

I desire to make it my earnest prayer to be fitted for events and prepared for Duty and I am not able to Dictate. I know not what is right and best, I think I can chearful leave it in the hands of an infinite wisdom to govern praying for peace and good order and that good may come out of evil in God's own time and manner."

"1787, January 18. Thursday morning Husband set out with sleigh to help the men to Springfield which are raised in this town for the support of government. David Johnson our Boy is gone and a great many others, and it looks as Dark as Night, a very great Army is coming from toward Boston, and some are collecting on the other side — it appears as if nothing but the immediate interposition of providence could prevent Blood — and there I think I can say I desire to leave it. The counsel of the Lord that shall stand. And my Husband got home that Eve, but he proposes to go soon — may I still say Amen."

"January 21. Mr. Hopkins Spoke very well upon the present Dark Day.

Monday morning Mr. Phelps set out for Springfield.

Tuesday eve — he came back.

Wednesday. Killed two oxen, set out with the meat could not get to Springfield, came back.

Thursday set out again, got back. The mob attempted to march into Springfield, the government fired the cannon killed four.

Friday morning one Lock (that has lived here ever since last April) set out with Mr. Phelps for Springfield. I hear they got in safe.

January 28. Mr. Hopkins preached Prov. 19 21.

This has been a confused day. The Mob in a large body at Northampton another party at Amherst. Just as the meeting was done, the Northampton Body came into the lower end of Hadley street marched through to Amherst. What will be the event none can tell. We hope in God's mercy. Just at dusk my Husband got home.

Monday. Gen. Lincoln came into Hadley with about three thousand men.

Tuesday. Mr. Phelps carried the children into town to see 'em."

" Saturday evening David Johnson and Joseph Lock came home from the Army."

" February 4th, Sunday a confused time the Troops marched last Eve, the stores and baggage this day. Monday Mr. Phelps set out with some loadings belongings to the Army, went to Petersham. Tuesday home."

" February 21st. Went to Hatfield to the funeral of one Walker killed by the insurgents; — he was buried with the Honours of War."

" March 2d. Dr. Porter, two gentlemen of the army."

" March 22d. Thursday. Fast-day called; but

not one word of fast in the Proclamation only Humiliation and Prayer. I view it and keep it as fast."

"March 24th. Mr. Phelps set out for Boston to do Business for a great number of the inhabitants of this Town respecting pay for quartering the soldiers here."

The visit of General Lincoln to Hadley, and its mention in the diary, are of moment to those of his descendants now living under the old rooftree.

A major-general in the war of Revolution, the intimate friend and trusted adviser of the great Washington, a statesman whose integrity was unimpeachable and whose morals were unsullied, he has been honored and revered by his own and succeeding generations. He was appointed the first minister of war, an office involving, at that time, much that was both delicate and difficult, but which he faithfully administered. In his other positions also, under government, he uniformly sought the highest good of the nation, making it paramount to any private interest or ambition.

In the period of tranquillity which followed the Revolutionary war and its subsequent disturbances, Charles Phelps found ample field for action in the affairs of the town and the Commonwealth. He was for many years a Representative at the General Court, a selectman, a justice of the peace. As commissioner of highways he traveled all over the countryside, laying out roads and superintending the construction of bridges. In the early days of the war he had sent supplies to Cambridge for the army, and frequently accompanied these expeditions. Even in middle age, a day's journey of sixty miles in the saddle was no fatigue to him.

We learn from the diary that his wife often accompanied him to Boston, when they traveled in their own chaise.

"February 15, 1787. Went to Cambridge. Drank tea at Mr. Gannet's."

It may have been with some idea of sending their son to Dartmouth that in 1788 they took a trip to Hanover. The visit was much enjoyed. She writes that they took tea at one of the professors' houses, were received with much attention, and "saw the curiosities."

Young Moses, who afterwards took the name of Charles for his father and paternal grandfather, was entered at Harvard, always at that time spoken of as Cambridge College. After graduating he studied law with Chief Justice Parsons, and married into his family. Visits from his parents at his Boston home were the occasion of a round of tea-drinkings among the new relatives, in Charles, Summer, and Tremont streets.

Two or three times Mrs. Phelps mentions that they "went to the Play."

Public affairs did not interfere with the Squire's care of his own estate. He had doubled the acreage, and as early as 1770 the property was rated highest on the list in Hadley, with one exception.

Various industries were carried on in connection with the farm. At the falls near by was a gristmill; a tannery stood at the foot of Pleasant Hill; there was a blacksmith's shop, with buildings for stabling, storage, etc.

In the river were extensive fisheries of salmon and shad.

1783, May 17th. Mrs. Phelps says: "Rode up to the fish place to see our fish."

It is said that at one time salmon were so plenty that the shad were of no account, and were thrown back into the water. It was even considered disreputable to eat them, as indicating poverty. Mr. Judd has an anecdote of a family who, when they were surprised at dinner by some visitor, hid the shad under the table.

There is another story, that Colonel Porter and his wife, being secretly fond of the dish, gave their negro man private instructions to put a shad under his coat and bring it away when no one was looking.

When shad rose in value they brought a penny apiece. The fishing place at Forty Acres was one of the principal on the river, and was the scene of much youthful gayety and life.

"As a means of transportation of goods, farm products, and lumber, the river was of much importance. In the early part of the season, almost every day would witness the floating down of one or more of those sleepy, easy-going structures called rafts, the only care necessary being to keep in deep water and go with the current.

How I did envy the delicious leisure of those lumbermen! They had indeed a few boards for oars, but they were of very little use, judging from appearances, as they glided past near us poor fellows sweating in the cornfields. But the 'fall-boats,' as they were called, were pretentious affairs. They were long and flat-bottomed, and carried a mast with two sails. If not picturesque, they gave life to the river, and we missed them when they were superseded by the railroad car.

Since recalling the incidents of early life connected with Mt. Warner, and comparing them with others associated with the Connecticut River, I have been impressed with the difference between them as factors in my life experience.

If there was an air of reticence and mystery about those wooded solitudes; if the life lived there was grave, uniform, and quiet,— the very reverse of this was true of the river. In the winter, indeed, it was cold and silent, not half as companionable as the forest, but in the summer season all its life was on the surface. It was lovely, sociable, or saucy, foaming with rage or rippling with laughter, as the wind and skies played with its caprices.

I think my earliest recollections connected with the river were in passing over the old arched bridge about one fourth of a mile below the house. It was not then considered safe to drive over it faster than a walk, but it was a beautiful object in the landscape, with its graceful arches reaching from pier to pier, the flooring following the course of the arches. And when at length they began to fall away one by one at intervals, its picturesque effects were rather heightened than otherwise.

It was said that when the bridge was finished, Dr. Lyman, of Hatfield, preached on the occasion, and delivered himself of the opinion that, in view of such improvement, the millennium could not be far in the future.

Speaking of the bridge reminds me of the sport of 'going in swimming,' as we used to call bathing.

The boys would join forces, and, since the river flats back of the house were not favorable for diving, we used to resort to the bridge. By swimming over to the first pier, a good diving-place could be found, and thither they would go like a flock of ducks, for it was deep water all the way over.

Before I had learned to swim, my brother used sometimes to want to carry me on his back over to the pier. I used to require the most solemn assurance he would not play me false, and he never did. So, persuading me to put my arms about his neck, he would launch out and carry me over to the pier. Likely enough he would tease me awhile with the fear I should be left there, but he never had a thought of that.

O simple, unhesitating, buoyant faith of childhood! How often have I since prayed that when called to make the passage from this to the world beyond, I may have a like trust in our Divine Elder Brother, that He would carry me safely over."

A description of the Forty Acres Farm, in its period of greatest prosperity, has often been referred to in local histories and biographies. It is to be found among the writings of Dr. Timothy Dwight, a grandson of Jonathan Edwards, who was born in Northampton. It is related that three Timothys in direct succession — Colonel Timothy, Major Timothy, and President Timothy — at one time all raked hay together in the same meadow.

Of Colonel Timothy, the story goes that he once threw a stone not only across the Connecticut at Northampton, at a point where it was forty rods from shore to shore, but thirty rods beyond, in all 1,165 feet.

Of President Dwight's early years it is told that he learned the alphabet at a single lesson, read the Bible fluently at four, and commenced the study of Latin at six. He entered Yale College in 1765, when he had just completed his thirteenth year. He became a tutor at the age nineteen, was later admitted to the ministry, and served as a chaplain in the Revolutionary war. After some years spent in teaching, during which he supported his mother and brothers and sisters, he became pastor of a Connecticut parish, and subsequently the successor of Dr. Stiles as president of Yale. His biographer says of him: —

"A nobler example of a well-balanced mind is not to be found, perhaps, than Washington. Dr. Dwight, with far more of the imaginative and brilliant than belonged to the Father of his Country possessed the same well-proportioned intellectual character for which he was distinguished." His influence over his pupils, of whom a large number became leading men, was very marked. Of his breadth of view in religious matters, unusual compared with many ministers at that time, the following anecdote is told: —

"A young clergyman, since one of the most distinguished in New England, called upon him; and to an inquiry which the doctor made concerning the state of religion in his neighborhood he replied, as an evidence of its being in a flourishing state, that the distinguishing doctrines of the gospel were faithfully preached. 'That is well,' replied the doctor, 'but are the *duties* of the gospel preached also?'"

Among his many works, one of those most interesting at the present day is the book of "Travels." This collection of letters contains descriptions of his journeys through New England and New York State at the close of the last century and the beginning of the present. It abounds in carefully noted observations on the country he visited, interspersed with items of biography and history; and reflections, which are most valuable as indicating the mind and temper of the writer. His descriptions are full and accurate.

In portraying the beautiful view from Mt. Holyoke, familiar to travelers, he says:—

"Meadows are here seen, containing from five to five hundred acres, interspersed with beautiful and lofty forest trees, rising everywhere at little distances, and at times with orchards of considerable extent, and covered with exquisite verdure. Here spread, also, vast expanses of arable ground, in which the different lots exactly resemble garden-beds, distinguishable from each other only by different kinds of vegetation, and exhibiting all its varied hues, from the dark green of the maize to the brilliant gold of the barley.

One range of these lots is separated from another by a straight road, running like an alley, from one to two miles in length, with here and there a brook or mill-stream winding through the whole.

A perfect neatness and brilliancy is everywhere diffused; without a neglected spot to tarnish the lustre, or excite a wish in the mind for a higher finish. All these objects united present a collection of beauties to which I know no parallel.

When the eye traces this majestic stream, meandering with a singular course through these delightful fields, wandering in one place five miles to gain seventy yards, inclosing almost, immediately beneath, an island of twenty acres, exquisite in its form and verdure, and adorned on the northern end with a beautiful grove, forcing its way between these mountains, exhibiting itself like a .vast canal six or eight miles below them, and occasionally reappearing at greater and greater distances in its passage to the ocean; when it marks the sprightly towns, which rise upon its banks, and the numerous churches which gem the whole landscape in its neighborhood; when it explores the lofty forests wildly contrasted with the rich scene of cultivation which it has just examined, and presenting all the varieties of woodland vegetation; when it ascends higher, and marks the perpetually varying and undulating arches of the hills, the points and crowns of the nearer and detached mountains, and the long-continued ranges of the more distant ones, particularly of the Green Mountains, receding northward beyond the reach of the eye; when, last of all, it fastens upon the Monadnock in the north-east, and in the northwest upon Saddle Mountain, ascending each at the distance of fifty miles, in dim and misty grandeur, far above all other objects in view, — it will be difficult not to say that, with these exquisite varieties of beauty and grandeur, the relish for the landscape is filled, neither a wish for higher perfection, nor an idea what it is, remaining in the mind.

Among the interesting objects in this neighborhood, the farm of Charles Phelps, Esq., about two miles north of this town, deserves the notice of a traveler. This estate lies on the eastern bank of the Connecticut River, and contains about six hundred acres, of which about one hundred and fifty are intervale, annually manured by the slime of the river.

The rest consists partly of a rich plain, and partly of the sides and summits of Mt. Warner, a beautiful hill in the neighborhood. The intervale is universally meadow, and of the best quality. The remainder of the farm is remarkably well fitted for every kind of produce suited to the climate, abounds in pasture, and yields an inexhaustible supply of timber and fuel. It is also furnished with every other convenience.

On one border are excellent mills; on another a river, furnishing a cheap transportation to market. It is intersected by two great roads, leading to Boston and to Hartford. A bridge crosses Connecticut River one fourth of a mile below the house. Within two miles is the church in Hadley. The country around it is highly improved, and the inhabitants inferior to those of few places of the same extent in their habits and character.

The scenery, both near and distant, is eminently delightful, and within very convenient distance all the pleasures of refined and intelligent society may be easily enjoyed. In a word this estate is the most desirable possession of the same kind and extent, within my knowledge."

President Dwight described Hadley and its surroundings with the familiarity of many years' acquaintance. A close relation, through the Edwards family, with Lawyer Porter's household, made him a frequent visitor. He was accustomed to preach for Mr. Hopkins, also a connection. Of one of these occasions we find that the family chronicle makes particular mention: —

"May 13, 1798. Mr. Dwight, Pres. of New Haven College, Lawyer Porter and wife (and others) all drank tea here."

By the dates we may conjecture that it was on this same visit to the old mansion that President Dwight became impressed with the beauty, virtue, and high character of the daughter of the house. Elizabeth Phelps was at this time nineteen years of age. There is a portrait which represents her dressed in a short-waisted white gown, her brown hair in a mass of curls on the top of her head; with dark eyes, a long upper lip, a firm chin.

The rude hand of the country artist failed to give that expression to the countenance which would endow it with soul and character, but the cast of feature marks unmistakably decision, will, refinement. There are also such striking points of resemblance to her descendants of the present day that one cannot doubt that the picture in its outlines was a faithful likeness.

From knowledge of her character as it developed in later years, one may read penetration in the eye, severity in the mouth, intellect in the brow. If there is latent melancholy in the expression, the light in the eyes betrays quick humor; the lines in the face indicate sympathy, aspiration, affection.

With the advantages of a trained mind, a cultivated taste, natural dignity, and the sprightliness of youth, it is no wonder that she made an impression upon the fancy even of an elderly college dominie. His estimate of her character, as it was afterwards expressed, is the more flattering because, in his visits to the metropolis, he finds occasion for extreme censure on the prevailing manners and conversation of the young people he met.

Returning, however, to New Haven, he not only recalled the attractions of Miss Phelps, but depicted them in glowing terms to one of his favorite tutors. Urging upon him the prudence of selecting a suitable helpmeet, he advised him to visit Hadley and seek an introduction to the Squire's daughter. For charm of person and of character he esteemed her without a rival.

That his advice should have been so favorably received, we know not whether to attribute to the respect which the young clergyman entertained for the opinion of his honored president, or to the effect made upon him by the picture drawn.

He was at that very time entertaining the offer of a parish in one of the prosperous Connecticut towns. Such a home needed a wife to complete its attractions. With the acceptance of the settlement, the young minister turned his attention to the selection of a companion. Six months after the tea-drinking, at which President Dwight was a guest, comes the following entry:—

January 13, 1799. "Mr. Huntington Pastor of Litchfield preached," and, a day or two after, "Mr. Huntington drank tea here."

In the next May, there was another visit from President Dwight, perhaps to offer congratulations on the becoming manner in which his counsel was received. It is said, however, that the young lady, with strict Puritan reserve, would never admit that there was an engagement. In spite of that, the parsonage at Litchfield was made ready, and the wedding took place New Year's Day, 1801, in the Long Room of the old house, where a party of relatives and friends were assembled. The journey to the new home was made through the snow in a sleigh. Teams were sent on before, containing the bride's belongings and the substantial outfit which her father provided for housekeeping.

After this, the diary records frequent expeditions to Litchfield. This town was the residence of many families of distinction, and noted for its refined and hearty hospitality. Tea-drinkings and other entertainments occurred with frequency in honor of guests from abroad. Names well known to this day in Connecticut are often found in the diary on the occasion of Mrs. Phelps's long visits at the parsonage.

From this time her private diary is supplemented by letters, in good preservation, written by the affectionate and anxious mother to her daughter. The anticipation of visits to Litchfield were always joyful. The journey from Hadley was once performed by carriage in a single day, but usually Mr. and Mrs. Phelps stayed over night with friends or relatives at Westfield or Hartford. In a season when the roads were very bad, it was taken partly on a pillion.

Returning home after the first visit to the young couple the month after the wedding: —

"February 7, 1801. Got home about twelve found all things very clever (but no Betsey) for which I hope we are very thankful."

Mrs. Phelps's home was now in many respects altered. Her mother had died two years before; her only son and an adopted daughter Thankful were both married. Her vigor of character, however, and her cheerful disposition, grew only more marked as old age came on and changes occurred. At the age of fifty-nine she writes after an illness : —

"Took physic and consulted the family physician all to no purpose; suspected the disorder to be nervous; tact'd about, put on great resolution, and made mince pies, and really found myself no worse than days before."

To her husband, whose mood was reserved and inclined to melancholy, she writes : —

"Your last seems a little low-spirited, the others do very well. I could feel in the dumps too, if I dare, but that will never do."

To her daughter: "Betsey, put on patience — let it have its perfect work — if you get extremely worn out perhaps I had better spel you awhile."

"Put on courage" was her favorite saying, and might have been her life motto. With advancing years she relaxed nothing of her native energy. When over sixty she rode to the top of Mt. Holyoke on horseback under the guidance of her son. She speaks of "the care of this great house and farm," and of rising with the dawn to superintend the butter-making in hot weather, of setting "forty dozen candles to dip," of making sausages and cheese.

In one absence, her careful mind sends the following charges to her husband: —

"There are two pies on the lower shelf in the old closet which you had better eat — and the key of the S. W. chamber is in my stocking drawer, at the S. W. corner, if you should have smart folks to lodge you might want it."

Visits from relatives and friends still occur with frequency.

On one occasion, somewhat earlier, we find recorded: —

"In the afternoon came above twenty visitors from ten different towns."

An old letter (1839) says: "Sometimes there seems to be a simultaneous movement among our friends and they come to us in swarms. Our company has been gradually accumulating until yesterday afternoon, when it became quite overwhelming. Our friends (I speak more particularly of the female part) seemed determined to come at all events, and if they could not get a man to drive, they would come without. Such a collection of chaises, buggies, and wagons of all descriptions you seldom see collected together. There were the old and young, the beautiful and the plain, the rich and poor, high and low, met together. I was told that two rooms were occupied for a considerable part of the afternoon."

FIREPLACE IN THE LONG ROOM

"The Mansion of our Forefathers," as Mrs. Phelps calls it, seems to have been always the scene of a generous hospitality. As the grandchildren grew up, they were warmly welcomed and tenderly cared for. The whole family of the son or daughter was often entertained.

Her simple nature seldom takes heed of anything worldly, but after a visit to Boston she writes to Betsey: —

"Daughter Sally has had her Aunt Parsons' bracelets sent her since her Aunt's death. The day before we came away she had her aunt's muff and tippet, cost $120 in Russia."

This and an allusion to the remodeling of a gown by a city dressmaker are almost the only references to outside appearance.

She frequently takes herself to task for short-comings in the control of temper and the performance of duties. A more wholesome, unaffected piety it would be difficult to find. Her interest in friends and neighbors never weakens; her solicitude for the members of her own household does not fail.

Sometimes, after a long and busy day, she sits down to write by the lamplight in the "Long-Room," where she may be undisturbed. Her husband, on such occasions, was away from home on business. One of his great interests connected with church affairs, in which he was always prominent, was the erection of a new meeting-house. Of this he superintended every detail, from the hauling of the lumber to the disposal of the pews.

The building is spoken of by President Dwight as a " handsome structure, superior to any other in this country."

It was afterwards removed from West Street to the Middle Street, where it now stands.

Among matters of general concern mentioned from time to time, we find the following reference to a peculiarly trying summer, that of 1805.

After a refreshing rain on August 1st she writes: —

" No rain to wet the ground from June 9th, eight weeks. Already the face of nature is changed. O God I thank thee, we feel our dependence, and now Lord may we feel gratitude."

Except for violent headaches, there is little mention of illness, and no indication of failing health up to the last date in the diary. That occurs 1812, April 5, Lord's Day.

"Thursday, Fast Day. Mr. Woodbridge. 2 Timothy 3, 1, 2, 3, & 4 verses. 'This know that in the last days perilous times shall come.' Satt. sent letter to Betsey."

Her death took place in November, 1817, at the age of sixty-nine. She survived her husband three years.

At the close of such a long and honorable life it is interesting to recall an anecdote told of her when only four or five years old: "During the last illness of her grandmother, the child was found alone in a retired room, repeating aloud the old hymn of which this is one of the stanzas: —

> 'Lord, if thou lengthen out my days,
> Then shall my heart so fixed be
> That I may lengthen out thy praise,
> And never turn aside from thee.'"

LATER LIFE IN THE OLD MANSION.

> I see . . .
> The hills curve round like a bended bow, . . .
> And round and round, over valley and hill,
> Old roads winding, as old roads will,
> Here to a ferry, and there to a mill;
> And glimpses of chimneys and gabled eaves,
> Through green elm arches and maple leaves, —
> Old homesteads, sacred to all that can
> Gladden or sadden the heart of man, —
> Over whose thresholds of oak and stone
> Life and Death have come and gone!
> J. G. WHITTIER.

By the year 1816 a fine family of sons and daughters was growing up in the Connecticut parsonage, but country salaries were in those days no more adequate than they are now to meet the increasing expenses of such a household. The minister himself thus describes his circumstances: —

"Here I am, then, planted down in social life with a fair prospect of usefulness, in a companionship every way conducive to domestic comfort and every earthly enjoyment. Happy could it have been continued. It was ordered otherwise. My dependence for support was the *settlement* ($1,000) and four hundred dollars salary. The offer was made before my leaving New Haven. My friends there told me I could never live upon it. I told them their promises at Litchfield were fair in case of insufficiency.

Doctor Dwight I remember told me a story, as he often did, of a Northampton man, I believe it was a Mr. Lyman. The man had a son much in the same predicament as I was. His father asked him if he could live upon the salary offered him. He replied, 'Father, the people are very able, and very generous; it is a country town; thirty or forty professional characters; schools of every grade; great geniuses among them; and they have been in the habit of making liberal presents to their former minister, and doubtless will continue them.' His father's reply was, 'Bind 'em, John.' 'They will supply me with firewood, father, as they have always been in the habit of doing for their minister,— of course.' 'Bind 'em, John.' 'But, father, they have to pay their former minister, now worn out with age and faithful services, his whole salary, which was only £100 ($333.33), from which they expect soon to be released, and which they say can just as well be added to mine as not if I survive.' The reply still was, 'Bind 'em, John.'

How it came out with John I cannot say. My own case, very similar, I shall not soon forget; and it will be well for us all not to forget the old proverb, 'A bird in the hand is worth two in the bush;' and another we all remember: 'They that wait for dead men's shoes may go barefoot.' For years, the support of my family was eked out by bountiful contributions from abroad, as well as at home, particularly from 'Forty Acres.'

My wife had parents, blessed be the memory of their generous souls! who from their abundance would not suffer their daughter for a day to live in want of comforts appropriate to her station, and which they were able to afford her. As the wants of an increasing family required, wagon-loads and sleigh-loads of things necessary to the body were sent us gratuitously, from year to year, above seventy miles. To say nothing of my own feelings, my people seemed too well pleased with it to suit my notion. I have ever felt bound to support my family honorably, and nobody that I ever heard of ever accused us of any extravagance. . . . Within a year from leaving Litchfield, I was settled in Middletown.

After trying awhile, without any particular misfortune, I found my income did not meet the expenses of an increasing establishment, in the style of city life.

I asked again for an honorable dismission, which I obtained without difficulty. I found a pleasant retreat on the patrimony of my wife. We came to Hadley to reside in 1816. Our mother, Mrs. Phelps, who had been a widow about two years, survived her husband from this time about as long."

For many years the old home was now overflowing with the vigor and gayety of young life. After the eldest had gone out into the world, the eleventh child was born, the youngest of seven sons who grew up to manhood.

Although the boys engaged in the work of the farm, they were all afforded excellent opportunities for study and attended the village academy, of which their father was for some years preceptor. Several were thus fitted for college. The daughters finished their education at that excellent establishment for young women, Mrs. Willard's seminary, at Troy. Like their brothers, however, they took their part in the homely duties of the household. One of their occupations is thus described : —

"Singing was a favorite pastime with the sisters, and as they had excellent voices they enlivened their work with song. They were good spinners on the large wheel, and used to have their regular morning tasks in spinning woolen yarn.

In the summer they used to place their wheels in the corn-house and make it sing with their music until it seemed as though every skein of the yarn had a thread of harmony woven into its very fibre.

I wonder if you ever saw the process going on

of spinning on the large wheel? As a gymnastic exercise merely, it was vastly superior to any modern invention. Dancing is vapid in comparison, because though a graceful exercise it is purposeless except as a selfish amusement.

Common gymnastics have a purpose, but as generally practiced the means and the end are so indistinct that many do not see it. But in this matter of spinning there is not only variety of movement, the unequal but measured tread backward and forward, and the independent action of each arm, but behind all there was the purpose which gave power to every movement. Very likely it was owing to the training of the large spinning-wheel, more than they imagined, that the matrons of a former generation were able to appear with grace and dignity in any sphere in which they may have been called to move."

When the eldest sister was to be married, her trousseau must be provided at home.

"I suppose the fitting a daughter with her marriage portion was quite a different thing when I was a boy from what it is now. In my sister's case the linen, and I presume the woolens also, were furnished from the farm.

I recollect very well going over to Northampton in company with brother T. to drive a fat ox which was to help pay for the outfit, and this payment was added to from time to time, if I am not mistaken, by other products of the farm.

My sister had the promise of all the flax and wool also, I believe, that she could spin, to be made into fabrics. I imagine this would not be considered much of an offer now as a part of a marriage portion, but it was gladly accepted by her, and I doubt if the little spinning-wheel ever knew a more busy season than that which preceded her wedding.

The old north kitchen was her workroom, and every sunrise of the week-days found her seated beside the wheel, her hair bound up tightly with a kerchief to keep out the dust, her foot upon the treadle with measured beat, her nimble fingers pulling the well-combed flax from the distaff, and giving it that nicety of touch which should make the thread fine and even, before the flyer should fasten upon it with its irrevocable twist and send it to the spool.

I used to rise early in those days, and many a morning my first visit would be to the north kitchen, for no reason but to catch sight of the earnest figure and be entertained by the lively hum of the wheel."

Besides the hours devoted to work and play, both boys and girls were encouraged at home in the cultivation of a literary taste. It was the custom to spend their leisure time in reading. They were constantly supplied with the standard works, and with publications of the day in different fields of writing,— theology, history, fiction, and biography especially. The size of the family and the distance from the village had a tendency to throw the children together for companionship, and also to lead them to seek resources in themselves. In this way the home life became a peculiarly happy one.

Of its simple pleasures one of them has written: —

"To a boy or girl on the farm, every day brings its fresh surprises. The new life in the shape of a young calf or lamb, or brood of chickens, is always a new joy, however often repeated, and in spring especially the love of color, form, and sound is ministered to by spring flowers, or hum of insects, or dash of butterfly, or plumage and melody of birds in endless succession. I recall at this moment some of the early summer mornings in Hadley. How changed from the night before! It was as if a new picture had been drawn by the Infinite Artist for my especial pleasure. Earth and sky are written over anew with the finger of God, and the world exults in sunlight and song. Each object has a beauty of its own, fresh, perfect, and inimitable. With me, too, this novelty pertains to the seasons no less than to the panorama of the passing days. I believe the first note of the robin or bluebird in spring even now awakens a thrill not less keen than it did fifty years ago.

Long before the house-fly tries its wings on

the kitchen window, or the clover-bud bursts its winter sheath, I feel as though I must anticipate the season by dabbling in a small way with plant life.

I imagine that some such subtle tie as this keeps alive the charm of rural life."

Especially associated with childhood on the old farm was the keeping of the annual Thanksgiving. "It was one of the days we reckoned by, the dividing line between summer and winter, as well as the days of reunions and festivities. The season's work, as far as the land was concerned, was expected to be done before Thanksgiving; and indoors, house-cleaning with its vexations must be well out of the way.

The winter supply of apple-sauce must have been made ere this. The apples from the Mt. Warner orchard had been laid up, and a generous quantity of the juice had been boiled down to the consistency of thin molasses, with which to sweeten the sauce, for our forefathers were economical.

The old cider-mill, which had been all the season screeching its protest against the sacrilegious use of one of Nature's best gifts by turning it into brandy, had uttered its last groan and stood with naked jaws and bending sweep, a ghastly spectacle, until another season should compel a renewal of its doleful cries. The apple-paring, with its array of tubs and baskets and knives and jolly faces before the bright kitchen fire, was completed, with the Hallowe'en games of counting the apple seeds, and throwing the paring over the head to see its transformation into the initials of some fair maiden.

The great day for the conversion of the apples into sauce had lately come and gone, for it must be delayed as long as possible, that it may not ferment and spoil. The stout crane that swung over the huge fireplace was loaded with one or more brass kettles filled with apples, sweet and sour in proper proportion, the former being put at the bottom because they required more time to cook. Sprinkled through the mass were a few quinces, if they were to be had, to give flavor, while over the whole mass was poured the pungent apple molasses which supplied the sweetening. The great danger was that the sauce should burn; and to prevent this, some housewives had clean straw prepared and laid at the bottom of the kettles, lest the apples should come in too near contact with the fire. It was an all-day process, but when completed an article was produced which was always in order for the table, and which, if slightly frozen, was enjoyed with a keener relish than the ice-cream of the restaurants of to-day.

I suppose every family has its own way of preparing for and keeping Thanksgiving, but possibly the children may be interested to know how their grand-parents kept it at their age. Truth obliges me to tell that it began, like the old Jewish Feast of the Passover, with a great slaughter, not of lambs, however, but of equally innocent chickens, and — must I confess it? — on the Sunday evening of Thanksgiving week. I can only say in palliation of this, that it was a religious feast, or, if that does not satisfy the humane instincts of the age, I will add that in those days Sunday was universally regarded as beginning at sundown Saturday and ending on Sunday.

Charles Dudley Warner says that, though this was the theory practically, as far as the young folks were concerned, and perhaps not altogether without example from their elders, the Sunday began at candle-lighting Saturday and ended at sundown the next day. But Warner, as we know, is a great humorist, and sometimes goes to the very verge of the actual to make a point; but, judged by his own representations, our fathers could hardly be called Sabbath-breakers because the hen-roosts were never allowed to be visited till after dark! Will the lawyers admit my defense?

Monday was devoted, of course, to the weekly washing, and nothing must interfere with that.

Tuesday was the great day for the making of pies, of which there were from thirty to fifty baked in the great oven that crackled and roared right merrily in anticipation of the rich medley that was being made ready for its capacious maw. Two kinds of apple pies, two of pumpkin, rice, and cranberry made out the standard list, to which additions were sometimes made. Then in our younger days we children each had a patty of his own. These were made in tins of various shapes, of which we had our choice, as well of the material of which our respective pies should be composed. The provident among us would put these aside until the good things were not quite so abundant.

Was not that a breath equal to the 'spicy breezes of Ceylon' that greeted us as the mouth of the oven was taken down, and the savor of its rich compounds penetrated every crevice of the old kitchen, like sacrificial incense? Then, as the pies were taken out and landed on the brick hearth, and a number of pairs of eyes were watching the proceedings with the keenest interest, it would not be strange if pies and eyes sometimes got mixed up. I remember once quite a sensation was produced in the little crowd because brother T. lost his balance, and, for want of a chair to break his fall, sat down on one of the smoking hot pies!

After cooling and sorting, the precious delicacies were put away into the large closets in the front entry or hall, which the foot of the small boy was not permitted to profane.

Wednesday was devoted to chicken pies and

raised cake. The making of the latter was a critical operation. If I mistake not, it was begun on Monday. I believe the conditions must be quite exact to have the yeast perform its work perfectly in the rich conglomerated mass. In due time the cake is finished. The chicken pies are kept in the oven, so as to have them still hot for supper. The two turkeys have been made ready for the spit, the kitchen cleared of every vestige of the great carnival that has reigned for the last two days, and there is a profound pause of an hour or two before the scene opens.

The happy meetings, the loaded tables, the hilarity and good cheer that prevailed, checked but not subdued in after years as one and another of the seats are made vacant by their departure to the better land, — these are things to be imagined, but cannot be described. Warner, in his 'Being a Boy,' says that the hilarity of the day is interfered with by going to meeting and wearing Sunday clothes; but our parents managed that wisely by dividing the day, the first half of it being kept religiously, but the afternoon being given up to festivity, — by no means, however, common week-day work. This was wise, I say, because it would be almost cruel to allow a lot of young people to indulge themselves to the very extent of prudence, to say the least, in eating, and then sit down to reading good books. This distinction between relaxation and toil for pelf is, I think, too often forgotten nowadays, founded as it is on both religion and philosophy. I remember well the sad look mother gave my brother and myself after our having spent the afternoon in making a hen-house, a very 'cute operation, we thought, but which found no favor in her eyes, as contrary to the traditions of the forefathers.

But the day after Thanksgiving, it must be admitted, had its peculiar pleasures. I doubt if there was any other of the holidays of the year when we boys felt so strongly the sense of freedom, and it was all the sweeter because it was the last we should have before we were set to our winter tasks. Skating was pretty sure to be one of the sports, if the weather had been cold enough to make the ice strong; and indoors there remained for our keen appetite the broken bits of pie and cake, to say nothing of the remnants of the turkey and fowl of the day before, and which were enjoyed with a keener relish, if possible, than at first.

I forgot in its more appropriate place to speak of the roasting of the turkey. This was done in a tin oven with an iron rod running through it, and also through the meat that was to be cooked. This was the spit. The meat was fastened to the spit with skewers, so that, by means of a small crank at the end, it could be made to revolve in order to cook evenly. The oven was in shape something like a half cylinder, with the open side to face the fire. But there was a still more primitive way of roasting a turkey, and one which was resorted to sometimes when our family was the largest. Room was made at one end of the fireplace, and the turkey was suspended by the legs from the ceiling, where was a contrivance to keep the string turning, and of course with it the turkey. On the hearth was a dish to catch the drippings, and with them the meat was occasionally basted. The thing is accomplished much more easily now, but at an expense, I imagine, in the quality of the work.

It is interesting to observe the universality of some of the customs that were in vogue fifty and one hundred years ago. In looking over the Centennial of the Churches of Connecticut, I came across the remark that the festive board, so crowded with good things on Thursday, gradually took on a plainer and less profuse array of dishes, until it ended off on Saturday evening with a simple bowl of hasty pudding and milk. This was in Revolutionary times; but fifty years later, when I was a boy, the same practices prevailed; in fact, hasty pudding and milk was the standing dish for Saturday evening, as boiled Indian pudding was for Sunday's dinner. I have been reminded since reading this item of a couplet my brother once repeated to me when we were boys: —

> 'For we know Northampton's rule to be
> Fried hasty pudding 'long wi' tea.'

Expressive, if not elegant, and it shows that Northampton, bating the slight innovation of the tea, was true to New England tradition.

The Christmas holidays, as they are now observed, were not known in the country towns then. New Year's presents were often made, and the 'Happy New Year' greeting was passed when neighbors met each other; but with most people we were too near the Puritan age to hear the 'Merry Christmas' so common to-day, without a shock as though it were a profanation.

But our mother seemed to be a kind of seer in this, as in some other things; and before the children were too old, St. Nicholas was a well-known personage, and the hanging of the stocking in a veritable chimney never proved an idle ceremony. The only legend she ever related to me that I remember concerning the birth of Christ was, that at midnight all the cattle in the yards or fields might be seen kneeling with their heads turned to the east in adoration of the wonderful Being who made a manger his cradle, as if in dumb worship they sought a reverential though it might be distant kinship to One who stooped so nearly to their humble condition. I remember the charm that with me attached to the story, and the unwillingness with which I gave up the illusion when she once told us that, in her eagerness to see for herself, she broke the charm by sitting up one Christmas eve with a companion until the spell-bound hour, and visiting the cattle-yard of her father. Is it not sad that one's faith should receive such rude shocks, even before its bounds are reached! For myself, I can only say that though since then I have cherished many a vision within the bounds of possibility, only to have it marred by the stern realities of life, there is none perhaps that I have given up more reluctantly than this sweet, simple legend of the dumb cattle kneeling in honor of the babe of Bethlehem."

The mainspring of such a family life was the mother. We have seen what she was in the bloom of youth, when her high order of mind and character attracted the admiration of President Dwight, and through him of her future husband. The promise of early womanhood was more than fulfilled in maturity.

Of the three Elizabeths in direct succession, one passed nearly half a century, the others more than that period, in the old homestead. All were carried over its threshold to their last resting-place in the village graveyard. The first, made a widow by early and sudden bereavement, lived ever after in its shadow. She instilled in her only child that stern sense of duty, that clear discernment between good and evil, that unwavering faith in a righteous Ruler, which she had inherited from her forefathers.

Her own grief seems not to have interfered with those obligations of hospitality and kinship which her position involved.

In her daughter the austerity of a rigid creed was softened by a strong devotional spirit, a large-hearted humanity, a buoyancy and hopefulness of disposition.

With the third Elizabeth the same Puritan austerity was perhaps accentuated by the inheritance of reserve and stern decision which came from her father's family. Mingled with this was a susceptibility and a self-depreciation inclined to melancholy. Hers was a nature responding quickly to all that was noble, easily depressed by anything false, tender and generous in its sympathies, severe and relentless in self-condemnation. An uncompromising moral sense, joined with the scrupulous Puritan conscience, led her to seek the attainment of the highest standard in herself and her family. A large benevolence made her lenient and pitiful towards the sinful and the suffering.

Her deep affection for her children, and her intense concern for their spiritual welfare, is apparent in her private writings.

The journal which she kept most of her life is almost entirely a record of her private feelings, prayers, and heart-searchings. It begins in her girlhood with a solemn covenant which was renewed every year. With the birth of her children their names are continually repeated, and solicitude for their spiritual welfare occupies her more and more.

"Her whole journal was studded with prayers, as the heavens are with stars. It seems sometimes in reading it as if the mere mention of one of our names was enough to kindle into flame the hidden fire that ever lived within her breast.

It is no small privilege to be able to call such a woman mother. I think, next to our great Advocate who is ever at the right hand of the Father to make intercession for us, in persistence and in power are the prayers of those who gave me birth, and I should not dare to say how far they may not reach, or the favors they may not secure.

I can only compare our mother to some faithful soldier to whom is committed the task of bringing the household of a king from a distant province through an unfriendly country to the capital of the empire, whose loyalty and devotion were so ardent that he would gladly give up his own life rather than that of those intrusted to his care should be lost. But she was not content with this: she would lay hold of those by the wayside, and, by the sweet compulsion of her prayers, compel them to be her allies and escorts.

If we speak of vigilance, persistence, or fertility of resource, of courage and endurance, Stanley's famous march through the African wilderness to the ocean was as much inferior to it as earth to heaven; and as she saw one after another enter the palace portals and vanish from her sight, she could say through blinding tears, 'Father, I thank thee.'"

Any chronicle of early New England life would be incomplete without taking note of a great religious change which passed over it during the first quarter of the present century. That its influence was felt even in a lonely farmhouse, by a woman of such intense character as Elizabeth H., is not remarkable. While her husband, through his ministerial associations, realized the quickening impulse of freer thought, she also in her spiritual communings sought for guidance in a gospel which preached love to man as well as love to God.

From the pulpit under which she had sat since childhood, there were weekly outpourings of anathema, fiery denunciations of the unconverted, dogmatic dissertations on the righteousness of the Almighty. But the story of the Reconciliation, of Him who became man for the sake of his brothers, was lost sight of.

The old Puritan faith had been grand in its unhesitating belief in a Ruler and Lawgiver, with the sense of personality which upheld the conscience in responsibility to its Maker. The later teachings from the lips of New England divines obscured this simple and direct creed by constantly dwelling on human depravity and the doctrines of a theological system which seemed to fetter the will itself. The vileness of the creature was indeed depicted with a view to exalt the majesty and sovereignty of God; the certain damnation of the wicked was a theme intended to enhance the future blessedness of the elect. But there were those whose love for God was best satisfied in performing deeds of mercy and charity towards man, and whose conception of salvation was not that of personal security. To such the terrors of judgment appealed little; trust in Heavenly Love was the mainspring of life. They longed to help the suffering, to break the chains of the slave, to bring peace and order to a distracted world.

The era of religious enthusiasm in which so many New England churches broke from the bondage of Calvinism was a period of activity in the cause of humanity. Here Elizabeth found her happiness and delight. The anti-slavery movement was to her more than sentiment. As a practical proof of her interest in the African race, she took a little black boy, not only under her care, but into her own sleeping-room.

She eagerly read and distributed the publications of the Peace Society. The beginning of the temperance agitation engaged her ardent sympathy.

When the change of view of so conspicuous a member of the Hadley congregation became known, she was subjected to rigid inquiry by the deacons. After many visits and repeated interrogations she was judged guilty of heresy, and her name stricken from the list of church members.

This exclusion from the table where her father and mother had communed could not fail to be a grief to one of so sensitive and conscientious a disposition. Her husband, as a clergyman, was under no such jurisdiction. Although often occupying pulpits in the neighborhood, where a more liberal creed had been adopted, he at other times accompanied his wife to the place of worship in Northampton which she continued to attend during the remainder of her life. Sorely as he and her children resented the unnecessary persecution of so good and noble a woman, they regarded it as the unhappy outcome of a perverted ecclesiasticism. In later years they returned to their old place in the village meeting, knowing that in spite of differences they were made welcome.

To the little library over the old porch, where the ancient volumes of Edwards, Wigglesworth, and other stern theologians long stood alone, new sermons and essays now found their way. Channing and Martineau, Ware and Dewey, were widely read in the awakening of new ideas.

The movement which they represented has passed away, like that form of Puritanism which preceded it. There is no "Brimstone Corner" now left in Boston, neither is there any society of religious teaching such as that of fifty years ago. Many of its followers returned to the mother church in which their English forefathers had been baptized; some joined the Roman communion; many have formed what are known as Liberal denominations.

As a phase of reverent religious belief, Scriptural in its foundation, broad and tender in its sympathies, elevating in its influence, the present generation owes a debt of gratitude to the school of Channing and his contemporaries. It distinctly inherited much that was noble in Puritanism. Its traces are seen in New England literature, in its philanthropy, its morality, in its social teaching. It may yet prove to have been the doorway into a Universal Church, and a step towards the realization of a true Brotherhood of Man.

The third Elizabeth lived to see her grandchildren growing up around her. She passed from earth on one of those fast days which she kept so strictly, the anniversary of her youthful self-dedication.

Her husband, who lived to the age of ninety-one, retaining to the last his genial disposition and kindly interest in all around him, wrote an account of his wife when past his eightieth birthday.

He says, speaking of her later years: —

"She was continually seeking out the poor,

the ignorant, the vicious and unhappy, in her district, and devising modest and efficient plans for their good. The latest designs she formed were for the moral and religious instruction of some destitute and colored children; and the last toil of her enfeebled hands was spent in preparing some article of comfort for an orphan.

Her final illness was painful, and continued more than a year. Her confidence in the Father's love was perfectly undisturbed. Her accustomed piety was too deep and too sincere to glimmer into any unnatural transports. Her strongest desire to be released from the agony of her disorder was uttered, after a weary night, in the words of the patriarch, 'Let me go, for the day breaketh.' Reminded of the loved ones who had gone before her, she replied, 'Oh yes! I shall look them all up.'

Her mental powers and accomplishments were of a high order. She had a rare ability in stamping her ideas on other minds. Through all her busy life, crowded with the cares of training eleven children, besides many voluntary engagements, she maintained a daily habit of reading the best books. She sang in an excellent, musical voice, and occasionally accompanied herself on the guitar.

One of the great privileges of her children was to gather about her, and hear her sing sacred songs on Sunday evenings, chief of which was the Bethlehem hymn, beginning, —

> 'When marshaled on the nightly plain,
> The glittering host bestud the sky.'

But, vigorous and active as her intellect was, her chief glory was her large and holy heart. She loved righteousness and truth better than any creed or sect. She loved those her Heavenly Father permitted her to call her own with a constancy and tenderness that no language can represent. She loved the Lord her God with all her soul; she loved her neighbor as herself."

In the family life of that time, the old home received a new name. Some letters of the daughters to their school friends are dated, playfully, "Vallée Douce," but as " Elm Valley " it has been known to the descendants ever since.

Nearly a century and half have passed since Moses Porter raised the roof-tree. Before his occupancy, only the cattle of the colonist or the foot of the red man trod its soil. Since he first tilled the fields, his title with that of his grandchildren and great-grandchildren has been maintained by that only which is of true value, — the use and development of its resources. Only what is of direct benefit to the community has been cultivated on its fertile acres, and the wild woodland has been left in all its beauty.

Another family mansion, dear also from association, stands on part of the original estate, which has gradually been divided and subdivided.

The ancient home has seen many come and

go. From the little child who last toddled over its doorway, back to the first of the line who crossed the threshold, eight generations may be counted. Could the old walls repeat the story of the life passed within them, it would be a record of simple habits, homely toil, godly conversation, gentle manners.

None of those who lived there desired greatly the world's riches, or the world's applause. They were content to serve their neighbors and the community with the same spirit in which their forefathers founded the new country. They have bequeathed to those who come after the best birthright, — an example of loyalty and virtue which it is in the power of each one to imitate.

APPENDIX.

An especial purpose of the foregoing collection was to preserve the descriptions of life in his boyhood, taken from letters of the late Theodore G. Huntington. Not long before his death in 1875, he wrote out these reminiscences for his niece, Mrs. J. P. Quincy, by whose permission they are published.

How strong was the affection inspired by the family home, appears from an extract taken from correspondence with his brother Edward, and dated Hadley, December, 1839: —

"Did you ever reflect upon the variety of scenes a house as old as ours must have witnessed since its erection? With me, it has been at times quite a fruitful subject of thought. I fancy that, if we could conceive it, to have kept a record of events as they transpired, it would furnish a volume rich in the history of human affections. All that is most bright and beautiful in existence, as well as its darker shades, have in their turn been found here. Childhood, ever active, inquisitive, and unsuspecting, has been here, as well as venerable old age; young and old, the grave and the gay, strangers and friends, have shared its hospitality; joy and sorrow have been frequent guests, though rarely seen together. Sickness and death have been here, too, casting a shade of sadness and gloom over the most cherished objects of life. The smile of welcome and the parting tear have followed each other; bridal wreaths and chaplets for the tomb have been woven in quick succession; occasions the saddest and most joyful have come and gone, like the shadows and sunlight over the landscape."

The third Elizabeth married the Rev. Dan Huntington, who was born in Lebanon, Connecticut, October 11, 1774. His mother, Bethia, was a direct descendant of Adrian Scrope, one of the judges who signed the death warrant of Charles I. On coming to this country he changed his name to Throop, which has been borne by the family ever since.

The children of Elizabeth Phelps and Dan Huntington were Charles Phelps, Elizabeth Porter, William Pitkin, Bethia Throop, Edward P., John Whiting, Theophilus Parsons, Theodore Gregson, Mary Dwight, Catherine Carey, Frederic Dan. The youngest and only surviving son is the present Bishop of Central New York. With his family he occupies his birthplace during the summer season.

The residence now know as the Phelps mansion, or Pine Grove, was built on the southern portion of the family estate in 1816, by the only son of Charles Phelps, Charles Porter Phelps. He removed his household from Boston the following year, and settled for the remainder of his life in his native place, where he attained a high reputation as an upright and honorable lawyer and a public-spirited representative. The house, still in good preservation, is the property of his children.

The facts relating to the early history of New Hampshire are taken from the " Phelps Memorial," prepared for his grandchildren by the late John Phelps, whose wife, Mrs. Almira Lincoln Phelps, was well known through her writings on education and science.